on track ...
Little
Feat

every album, every song

Georg Purvis

sonicbondpublishing.com

Sonicbond Publishing Limited
www.sonicbondpublishing.co.uk
Email: info@sonicbondpublishing.co.uk

First Published in the United Kingdom 2022
First Published in the United States 2022

British Library Cataloguing in Publication Data:
A Catalogue record for this book is available from the British Library

Copyright Georg Purvis 2022

ISBN 978-1-78952-168-9

Typeset in ITC Garamond & ITC Avant Garde
Printed and bound in England

Graphic design and typesetting: Full Moon Media

Thanks to ...

Stephen Lambe, once again for the opportunity to write this book, and for inadvertently challenging me to listen to Little Feat's entire discography.

Mark Costello, for immediately singing 'Gimme A Stone' when I told you I was working on a Little Feat book, which took me by surprise, as it was one of the last of their songs I would've expected anyone to know. It surprised me so much that it changed my attitude – for the better! – on writing about the post-Lowell years.

The gentleman whose name I didn't catch from Pilgrimage Records, for selling me *Thanks, I'll Eat It Here*, *Feats Don't Fail Me Now* and *Down on the Farm* at the East Falls record drop, and for saying you'd buy the book. If you did, I hope you recognize yourself here. Thanks for helping me complete my Feats collection!

Scott Armstrong, Patrice Babineau, Hugh, Lori, Edward McGovern, Olivia Miller, Bill Ransford, and Eric Zerbe, for your continued enthusiasm and support.

My parents, Lynn and Georg, for the introduction, and never asking why your Little Feat collection slowly shrank over time (and to my sister Leah, who didn't care but had to endure discussion about it against her will).

Spencer and William, for distracting me, except when I didn't want to be distracted.

And to Meredith: 'I have dined in palaces, drunk wine with kings and queens/But darlin', oh darlin'/ You're the best thing I've ever seen.'

Foreword

When I started formulating the outline for this book, it was going to have ten chapters and a postscript. I had no intention of writing about the post-Lowell-George Little Feat, as I simply had no interest in it. I'd heard some of the songs on the third disc of *Hotcakes and Outtakes*, and even listened to *Chinese Work Songs* when it was first released, and found it enjoyable enough, but none of the songs captivated me in the way that the Lowell-George-era songs had. I would much rather have listened to *Dixie Chicken* or *Waiting for Columbus* – and besides, I was a seventeen-year-old whose musical taste buds hadn't yet fully developed. Over time, my horizons broadened, yet I still believed Little Feat's best years ended on 29 June 1979. When I pitched the idea for this book to Stephen in April 2021, he was enthusiastic but said I'd have to cover their whole discography (This was unprompted by him – he'd had no idea of my initial intentions). Figuring I could probably conjure up a positive sentence or two for an additional 108 songs (including one I didn't know about and a fresh release midway through writing), I agreed and queued up their most recent album *Rooster Rag* to see what kind of an uphill battle I was going to have.

As I walked around my neighborhood – earphones on and phone at the ready for notes – I had a flashback to my Elvis Costello book, which, due to his extensive output, had to be limited to just his decade with The Attractions. I recall being disappointed that I couldn't get into his really interesting later stuff, but I recognized that his best-known material fell within the period of the book. In the final postscript paragraph, I wrote, '…there are those fans who insist that his best work is behind him … To those fans, I hope you enjoyed this book, but I also hope you'll give some of his later works a chance.' As I'd just re-read the book for a final edit before going to press, these words were fresh in my brain. I realized that I had to practice as I'd preached: I dug into the post-Lowell years and found myself pleasantly surprised, and even grew a new appreciation for the latter-day lineups.

This book explores Little Feat's recorded output from 1969 to 2021 – fifteen studio albums, one live album, a collaborative album, a fan-favored farewell record, and Lowell George's lone solo album: recorded reluctantly so he could get an advance for his band to stay afloat. Regrettably, that means Little Feat's live performances (which were, and still are, the stuff of legend) will be mentioned only in passing. This was a tough decision to make, as I've listened to hundreds of hours of Little Feat concerts, and each one is a unique experience. But an analysis of their shows really does deserve a book of its own.

on track ...

Little Feat

Contents

Introduction

Lowell George and Bill Payne met in the summer of 1969 when Payne – fresh from San Francisco – decided he wanted to join Frank Zappa's Mothers of Invention. Using a fake calling card, Payne got through to the receptionist at Bizarre Records, who gave him Lowell George's information instead. George had joined The Mothers in November 1968, but a song he wrote called 'Willin'' got him kicked out, and he was now forming his own band. Payne met up with George at his house, and after the two hit it off, further meetings were initiated (and also recording sessions for George's then-current band Fraternity of Man). Before long, Payne forgot about wanting to join The Mothers, instead wanting to join forces with George. Payne later recalled to Bud Scoppa in the *Hotcakes and Outtakes* box set liner notes:

> We talked about the kind of band we wanted it to be. Should we have a horn section? What should the bass player play? Are we going to relegate ourselves to one style of music? We decided there shouldn't be any limits to what we would do. If we wanted to play a waltz, great. If we wanted to play a straight-ahead song, fine.

The next step was to recruit the right musicians. Richie Hayward – George's earlier compatriot in The Factory and currently in Fraternity of Man – was drafted as drummer, while George's friend (and bandmate in the former) Martin Kibbee came in as bass player. But, 'Before the group was actually signed, I quit or was fired,' Payne told Scoppa. 'In other words, I couldn't agree with Lowell about him being the ultimate leader.' Indeed, George had appreciated Zappa's approach to running a band, deciding initially on an autocratic group: George would write the songs and lead the group, though others were eventually encouraged to contribute their own material.

Paul Barrère – another friend of George's – was then auditioned as bassist, against his wishes:

> Lowell showed up at my place, handed me his bass and said, 'Be at this address tomorrow. You're gonna audition as a bass player.' I said, 'Lowell, I've never played the bass. I'm a guitar player'. He said, 'Well, it's got two less strings – how hard can it be?'

When Barrère showed up, he was given the chart for a song called 'The Dance Of The Nubile Virgin Slaves', which had multiple time signatures and key changes. Unsurprisingly, he failed the audition, though his talent was not forgotten.

After a period of trying some other bassists (Hayward later recalled around fourteen or so auditioning), former Mothers bassist Roy Estrada was drafted, completing the line-up. Stuck for a band name, inspiration came from Mothers drummer Jimmy Carl Black, who noticed George's small shoes and said, 'Man, you got ugly little feet.' The fledgling band's road manager Rick Harper noted it *would* be a good band name, and suggested altering the spelling to 'feat': a subtle nod to George's pop heroes, The Beatles. In Ben Fong-Torres' excellent Little Feat biography *Willin'*, Patte Stahlbaum – Hayward's sister-in-law and George's first wife – said their pot dealer was the one who noticed George's tiny trotters and coined the name. Either way, it was certainly a better name than the then-current front-runner: Lyle Gleep.

In need of a record label, George and Payne dug into their songs for some demos, with four from The Fraternity of Man's aborted second album – 'Crack In Your Door,' 'Juliet,' 'Teenage Nervous Breakdown' and 'Framed' – set aside specifically for Zappa's manager Herb Cohen. Two further songs were submitted – 'Truck Stop Girl' (one of the first Payne/George co-writes) and 'Willin'.

The six songs written and recorded so far (a handful of unrecorded titles are known to exist) displayed a unique approach. George was the primary mover (Payne – as determined a songwriter but not as prolific – would serve mostly as collaborator on the first three albums), showcasing his unique 'cracked mosaic' writing approach – instead of conventional forms (like verse/chorus/ verse/chorus/bridge) in conventional time signatures, he explored off-kilter and syncopated rhythms, throwing in deliberate surprises. George later famously told *ZigZag* magazine: 'I use tape like someone would use manuscript paper.'

'Willin'' got the most attention, simply because of the controversial phrase 'weed, whites and wine' – tame by today's standards, but in 1969, words like 'weed' and 'whites' were simply not used in songs. As out-there as Zappa was, even *he* drew the line somewhere – he'd suggested George go off and form his own band, which eventually snowballed into claims that George was fired because of Zappa's disapproval of the lyrics, or that George was caught smoking weed when he knew of Zappa's zero-tolerance policy towards drugs. Whether Zappa fired George because of the song's subject matter or because he saw creative potential in him is up for debate – It's difficult to imagine 'Willin'' in The Mothers' repertoire, simply because it was completely at odds with what they were recording at the time.

With a handful of songs ready, Payne and George approached Atlantic Records president Ahmet Ertegun, who rejected the band for being too diverse. Undeterred, the two went to Burbank for a meeting with Warner Bros. Records A&R man Lenny Waronker. Instead of playing a tape for him, Payne sat down at a piano with George on acoustic guitar. Payne later told Scoppa that they performed 'eight or nine songs, all of which would end up on the first album,' and Lenny said, 'You've got a deal.' It was sort of like going to Schwab's Pharmacy and being discovered on a barstool.'

Little Feat (1971)

Personnel:
Lowell George: vocals, lead, rhythm and slide guitars, harmonica
Richie Hayward: drums, vocals
Bill Payne: piano, keyboards, vocals; lead vocal on 'Snakes On Everything' and
'Takin' My Time'
Roy Estrada: bass, vocals
Additional personnel:
Ry Cooder: bottleneck guitar on 'Willin'' and 'Forty Four Blues/How Many More
Years'
Kirby Johnson: string and horn arrangements
'Sneaky' Pete Kleinow: pedal steel on 'I've Been The One'
Russ Titelman: percussion, backing vocals; piano on 'I've Been The One'
Recorded at United Western Recorders, Hollywood, 15 July-31 August 1970; The
Record Plant, Los Angeles, 7 August-16 October 1970 – Except 'I've Been The One,'
'Willin'' and 'Truck Stop Girl' at the Village Recorder, Los Angeles, October 1969;
'Crack In Your Door' at the Village Recorder, Los Angeles, April 1970
Producer: Russ Titelman
Release date: US: January 1971
Peak position: US: -
Running time: 33:15

In July 1970, the band entered United Western Recorders to record their first
album, with George's friend Russ Titelman producing. The two had entered
into a publishing deal, even though George had already started Naked Snake
Music with Martin Kibbee. 'Willin'' was one of the first songs to be sent around,
with Linda Ronstadt taking a liking to it and recording her own version; as
did The Byrds, though their recording remained unreleased until an archival
reissue of their 1970 *(Untitled)* album. With four songs recorded and ready
to go, seven more were cut over the next three months, with further sessions
taking place at The Record Plant in Los Angeles.

The sessions ran fairly smoothly until tensions between George and Titelman
threatened the album's release. Titelman told Ben Fong-Torres that 'It became
rather contentious toward the end. I think Lowell … saw it differently and
wanted it to be a different record. Close to the end, we were fighting.' While a
publishing deal gone awry was blamed, Titelman maintained their falling-out
was due to money, creative differences, and control: the band had gone over
budget, and Titelman's vision didn't align with George's.

With their relationship spiraling, George injuring himself in a bizarre
accident only added to the stress: a gas-engine-powered model's propeller
cut up his left hand. As a result, he lost sensation in two fingers, Ry Cooder
then drafted in to play bottleneck on the Howlin' Wolf medley 'Forty-Four
Blues/How Many More Years.' (There was a positive outcome to George's
accident: He was forced to adapt and develop his bottleneck abilities in spite

of the injury, and – with his choice of slide being a Craftsman 11/16' spark plug puller instead of a traditional glass slide – developed a most distinctive technique that would be matched by others but never bettered.)

Midway through the sessions, Little Feat's debut single was released, earning rare praise from *Rolling Stone*'s Ed Ward, who called 'Hamburger Midnight' a 'masterpiece' and 'perhaps the best record I've heard in several months.' While he favored 'Strawberry Flats', Ward (rightly) credited himself with getting some momentum behind Little Feat. He told NPR's Terry Gross in 2014:

> I wrote that I hoped an album was in the works. Right off, I got a call from the press guy at Warners – 'Do you really think they're that good?' he asked, adding that he hadn't listened to it. I told him he should. And he said they'd been signed to make the single as a favor to someone, and then hung up to check if the option had been picked up. It soon was.

The album was finished by October, though Warner Bros. inexplicably sat on it until January. By that time, Little Feat had made their live debut (Christmas Day 1970 at Cincinnati's Reflections Club) and had gone off on a grueling and emotionally-taxing tour, on which a particularly mentally-fragile Payne was convinced that Warner Bros. was sabotaging the band to instigate a breakup so that Hayward could be recruited for Ry Cooder's band. Things almost immediately got better for Payne a few nights later in New York City, when road manager Rick Harper introduced him to the wonderful world of groupies – which not only helped with much-needed tension release but also provided the inspiration for future songs.

'Snakes On Everything' (Bill Payne)

First Hayward finds the groove, then George slides in on bottleneck guitar. Once Payne joins on lead vocal and piano, *Little Feat* is off running at a moderate, slinky pace. Unusually, the album kicks off with a song by Payne, not George – who had assembled the band and was its self-appointed leader – but it's still an effective opener, incorporating the album's general elements – goofy, nonsensical titles, absurdist if not downright absurd lyrics, and a fascination with syncopated rhythms, weird arrangements and marginal accouterments. (In a 2019 interview with jambase.com, Payne explained the title: 'There was a song called 'Thanks For Everything' that – based on the way I said it – became 'Snakes On Everything' to Lowell.')

The arrangement was given a lot of consideration, with angelic harmonies and horn blasts punctuating George's double-tracked bottleneck. While overall the song is a triumph, the finest moments are in the final 30 seconds, when George stretches for the guitar neck's upper reaches while Hayward flails wildly behind him; Payne keeping the chaos under control as the song fades out.

'Strawberry Flats' (Bill Payne, Lowell George)
US B-side (WB-7431), 16 September 1970; US B-side (WBS-49841), 23 September 1981

Poor 'Strawberry Flats.' Despite being the album's closest to a potential radio hit, it was relegated to the B-side of the weird and significantly less commercial 'Hamburger Midnight'. Over a decade later, it ended up on *Hoy-Hoy!*, and was once again forgotten and slipped out as the B-side of 'Gringo.' But this propulsive, mid-tempo rocker – from Payne's melodic piano to Hayward's tub-thumping drums to George's stream-of-consciousness travelogue where the already road-weary and battered narrator stops by a friend's house in Moody, Texas (Payne's birthplace), only to be turned away for his freakish hippie appearance – deserved better. 'Strawberry Flats' exemplifies not only how uniquely mature the early Little Feat songwriting was, but how George and Payne could come up with gold under duress after Atlantic Records president Ahmet Ertegun had rejected their early demos.

'Truck Stop Girl' (Bill Payne, Lowell George)
The most overt country/rock fusion on the album so far, this mashes the earthiness of The Band with just the right amount of tongue-in-cheek Rolling Stones parody. It's another concise two-and-a-half-minute tale on George's favorite subject – life on the road as a trucker – but with a twist: distraught by the titular character ending their affair, the trucker jumps back into his load 'without tightening down/It was a terrible thing to see what remained/Of the rig that poor Danny was in.'

Known to have been performed live only once in Lowell George's lifetime (11 February 1972 in Buffalo, New York), 'Truck Stop Girl' became a live favorite after Little Feat's 1988 reformation and appeared regularly in setlists from 1992 onwards.

'Brides Of Jesus' (Bill Payne, Lowell George)
The album descends further into weirdness with this, the most atypical song in the entire Little Feat catalog. It eschews conventional storytelling, instead relying on oblique biblical imagery, Payne's superbly lyrical piano and an overwhelming orchestra heavily dominating the arrangement. Payne and George would never write another song like it – which is a shame, as it's an interesting diversion that could've been explored and fleshed out further.

'Willin'' (Lowell George)
This is undoubtedly George and Little Feat's best-known song, and the one that put him on the radar as a songwriter of note. But this isn't the best-known recording. The version here is George's original publishing demo with Ry Cooder on slide guitar, though George told *ZigZag*'s Andy Childs in January

1975 that a more-fleshed-out demo also had The Byrds' Gene Parsons on drums and Russ Titelman on piano.

As a performance, 'Willin'' is perhaps a bit too straightforward; sung in George's natural voice and taken at a surprisingly strident pace, with George racing through the nefarious 'weed, whites and wine' line. That the song sounds like an earnest pastiche does the performance no favors. George believes the lyrics; he just sounds like he's on the verge of breaking into a smirk after each line. Cooder's accompaniment is competent if superfluous (he would make a greater impact on the album's Howlin' Wolf medley), adding little to George's performance.

George was later displeased with the recording, returning to the song on the next album, where a small but significant rearrangement would transform the song's tentative origins into its definitive statement as a lonely trucker anthem.

'Hamburger Midnight' (Lowell George, Roy Estrada)
US A-side (WB-7431), 16 September 1970

This is a downright greasy and juicy song, with George's nasty bottleneck matched in tone only by his sneering vocal, while Payne and Hayward plod away behind on piano and drums. George crams some *audio vérité* into the middle, where the band chat away about liquor stores and Big Macs. Otherwise, this is another life-on-the-road song about cars, trucks and girls.

'Hamburger Midnight' was an early live favorite, appearing sporadically in setlists as late as 1975, and was even performed occasionally in 1989, with two further performances in 2014 and 2020.

'Forty-Four Blues/How Many More Years' (Roosevelt Sykes/ Chester Burnett)
The influence of Chester 'Howlin' Wolf' Burnett on Lowell George can not be understated. Wolf was limited in his instrumental abilities, being more of a performer, which resonated far deeper with George. While he picked up and adapted some of Wolf's traits – stretched notes across bars – it was simply Wolf's presence that appealed to George. After catching Wolf in concert in Santa Monica, George approached his idol, pouring his heart out about how much he meant to him, only to be answered with a cold 'Fuck you'. George made varied retellings of this story in concert, but would wear the encounter as a badge of honor; so important was Wolf's influence on George that he was more likely to collaborate with musicians if they knew of Wolf. (Incidentally, Van Dyke Parks later cited Wolf as his favorite blues singer.)

This medley of two of Wolf's better-known songs is inspired, with Payne's steady piano, Hayward's unique drum rhythm (Like Wolf's original, he emphasizes the first beat of each measure instead of the more typical second and fourth offbeats) and George's gritty vocal and overblown harmonica. Once again, Ry Cooder helps out on bottleneck, though George also plays rhythm guitar: which is more prominent in 'How Many More Years.'

'Crack In Your Door' (Lowell George)

Another arrangement influenced by The Band, this tells the story of a hapless lothario chased from his girl's bedroom by her enraged parents, and has some truly evocative imagery for good measure:

> And I can still see her mother with her hair up in rolls
> As she cast a telling glance at that young girl's red-hot eyes

The arrangement packs a lot into its concise running time, with Payne's barrelhouse piano and Hayward's drums adorned with a boozy trumpet and George's particularly stinging bottleneck.

An early version recorded at Hollywood's TTG Studios on 22 July 1969 featured Elliot Ingber on guitar and was released on the 1993 compilation *Lightning-Rod Man*. Two additional tracks – 'Teenage Nervous Breakdown' and 'Juliet' – were recorded at this session, both of which, like 'Crack In Your Door,' were updated for the future albums *Sailin' Shoes* and *Dixie Chicken*, respectively.

'I've Been the One' (Lowell George)

This plaintive ballad – a heartbreaking yearning for a love that's ended – swaps Payne for producer Russ Titelman, who plays piano, adding 'Sneaky' Pete Kleinow on pedal steel. A sophisticated accompaniment of horns and strings adds color without overwhelming the performance, while George's vocal delivery poignantly wavers between wistful and determined.

'Takin' My Time' (Bill Payne)

Payne follows George's weepy ballad with one of his own, performed solo with orchestral accompaniment. It's a stately affair, showcasing Payne's superb mastery of his instrument while also displaying a mature handle on songwriting, even if he would go on to write better songs. 'Takin' My Time' was known to be performed live only once: on 7 January 1971 in Ann Arbor, Michigan.

'Crazy Captain Gunboat Willie' (Bill Payne, Lowell George)

The album concludes with the most eccentric song in the Payne/George backlog. It was edited down from a lengthy fourteen-minute semi-improvised piece (uploaded to the official Little Feat account on archive.org) to a little under two minutes, with a superbly outlandish brass arrangement. Mixing the majestic psychedelic pop of Procol Harum with the salt-of-the-earth character sketches of The Band, this unique diversion is a testament to Little Feat's off-

15

kilter sense of humor. While the song – like many on the debut – was likely a staple of the band's early repertoire, only one live performance is known of – meaning the attendees of their concert on 4 May 1971 at Geneva College in Beaver Falls, Pennsylvania, were lucky enough to witness it.

Related Tracks
'Jazz Thing In 10' (Bill Payne, Lowell George, Richie Hayward)
Recorded at the Village Recorder, West Los Angeles, 31 October 1969. Produced by Richard Moore and Michael O'Bryant.

This discordant instrumental was laid down at the pre-Warner-Bros. sessions in October 1969, with Bill Charlton on bass and George on saxophone. In the *Hotcakes and Outtakes* liner notes, Hayward called it 'outside stuff for the times,' and that's an understatement. It's an interesting listen, but George's performance is too free-form and grates almost immediately.

'Rat-Faced Dog' (Bill Payne, Lowell George)
Recorded at the same session as 'Crack In Your Door', this was later released on the *Hotcakes and Outtakes* box set. Its exclusion from the debut is understandable – while it's no worse than anything else on the album, it does ramble and occasionally struggles to find direction. Still, it's worth a listen.

'Doglines' (Bill Payne)
This fully-formed outtake would've been a worthy addition to the debut album if only it wasn't so structurally similar to 'Snakes On Everything'. The song was inspired by a profane dance move of Payne's high school classmates in Ventura: 'a dance that was certainly banned in Boston if it ever got that far!' The track was released in 2000 in the *Hotcakes and Outtakes* box set.

'Wait Til The Shit Hits The Fan' (Bill Payne, Lowell George)
This early performance of the *Feats Don't Fail Me Now* favorite was later released on the *Hotcakes and Outtakes* box set. While it's a fascinating insight into the song's genesis, the performance is far too tentative, proving that some songs just need time to marinate before they're ready.

Sailin' Shoes (1972)

Personnel:
Lowell George: vocals, guitars, harmonica; baritone saxophone and rhythm box on 'Cold, Cold, Cold'
Richie Hayward: drums, percussion, vocals
Bill Payne: piano, Wurlitzer electric piano, Hammond organ, accordion, vocals; lead vocal on 'Cat Fever'
Roy Estrada: bass guitar, vocals
Additional personnel:
Ron Elliott: rhythm guitar on 'A Apolitical Blues'
Milt Holland: percussion on 'Easy To Slip' and 'Trouble'
'Sneaky' Pete Kleinow: pedal steel on 'Willin'' and 'Texas Rose Café'
Debbie Lindsey: backing vocals on 'Cold, Cold, Cold' and 'Sailin' Shoes'
Recorded at Sunwest Recording Studios, Hollywood, 7-14 April 1971; Amigo Studios, North Hollywood; Sunset Sound Recorders and TTG Studios, Hollywood, 8 December 1971-6 February 1972
Producer: Ted Templeman
Release date: US: February 1972
Peak position: US: -
Running time: 37:44

With only 11,000 copies sold, *Little Feat* hadn't set the charts on fire, yet critics (at least those who noticed) adored the band. Luckily for them, so did Warner Bros. – or, more specifically, Van Dyke Parks, who went into bat for the band when the label refused to finance a follow-up. Parks had known George since the recording sessions for Fraternity of Man's second album, ultimately finding a kindred spirit in him. The two men worked together infrequently afterwards – Parks helping George out by including the newly-written 'Sailin' Shoes' (their first co-write) on his second album *Discover America*. Not that George wasn't trying for himself – desperate for another shot, he wrote 'Easy To Slip' with Martin Kibbee: a deliberate attempt at a hit single. (Warner Bros. was so impressed with it, they pitched it along with 'Texas Rose Café' to The Doobie Brothers, who opted against recording the songs.)

In the end, Warner Bros. re-signed the band. Little Feat had friends in high places, and with other out-there labelmates like Captain Beefheart and Frank Zappa – not to mention Parks himself – the band were in no danger of being dropped. After their first North American tour concluded in September, they went back into the studio, this time at Warner's Amigo Studios in North Hollywood. With the friendship of George and the first album's producer Russ Titelman now nonexistent, Ted Templeman was recruited as producer, with Donn Landee as engineer.

George dominated this album's songwriting, with seven of his own and one with Kibbee. Payne wrote the other three: two on his own (George arranging 'Cat Fever') and one with Hayward.

For George, the desire to experiment was great, and he used the studio as a canvas. With Templeman a willing participant, the two created an aural landscape that was just a little left-field. Templeman told Ben Fong-Torres: 'I was lucky to have an inventive group ... Lowell was great because we had a personal relationship, and he would ask my opinion all the time.' Not only did George have a particular sound in mind for 'Cold, Cold, Cold,' he also wanted to use part of his original demo on the finished recording. Templeman later told Bud Scoppa:

> The drum sound was something we came up with over at Sunset Sound using a little weird room that used to be a meat storage locker. It was Lowell's idea to use that stupid little drum machine of his, the Donca Matic. That way, when the drums came in with all that compression, it obliterated them.

A small group of guest musicians added some sparkle to the basic tracks, but *Sailin' Shoes* was a largely band-driven affair, and was more in line with George's initial vision of Little Feat than the debut had been. Released in February 1972 – mere weeks after the sessions wrapped up – *Sailin' Shoes* introduced to the fold another Little Feat auxiliary member. Neon Park – born Martin Muller – was an artist and comic illustrator who'd designed Frank Zappa's *Weasels Ripped My Flesh* album cover (which was how George and Park met). Park's style appealed to what Van Dyke Parks later called 'cartoon consciousness.' He later told Bud Scoppa:

> The guy would bifurcate just about everything so that you could listen to things on two different levels. I think he had the audacity of a schizophrenic, which I associate with great work ... I think Lowell had a madness in his work that he wanted to explore, and he had the integrity to do it.

George recognized his visual artist friend's sense of humor immediately in the cover for *Sailin' Shoes* – an attractively decorated anthropomorphized cake, swings on a swing, kicking off one red heel. She has a slice cut out of her – a not-so-subtle entendre – while a snail watches her from the front, and Mick Jagger peers over from behind, the beautifully manicured grounds blending into sky. On the back cover, the songs are listed in an alternate running order, though they're correct on the vinyl and the interior. The gatefold sleeve contains a series of band photos, the lyrics, and liner notes from George: all written in lowercase, in a rambling style that would come to define subsequent Little Feat albums. Titelman was given an arch credit – 'May he remain calm...,' and a crew of groupies known as the Houston Reception Committee were given a sly nod: in addition to inspiring 'Tripe Face Boogie' and 'Texas Rose Café.'

Once again, the album faltered, despite Scoppa's solid *Rolling Stone* write-up:

Rather than telling stories in a literal sense, Little Feat's songs flash a myriad of fleeting, haunting images, appearing with all the vivid suddenness of floodlit roadside billboards zooming past an open car window.

With *Sailin' Shoes* selling a mere 13,000 copies, the band's future was again in doubt: Warner Bros. had given them a second chance, but they weren't likely to give them a third. For the time being, it didn't matter – the album release coincided with another tour, and with this one being a more positive experience all 'round, it provided George with an opportunity to further expand his vision for Little Feat.

'Easy To Slip' (Lowell George, Martin Kibbee)
US A-side (WB-7553), 5 January 1972; US A-side (WBS-49801), 5 August 1981

Sailin' Shoes' most commercial song has an introduction reminiscent of the stark acoustic guitar/drums combination of The Rolling Stones' 'Street Fighting Man.' (An earlier February 1971 demo for the Doobie Brothers (known as 'Easy To Fall') was even more Stones-esque.) From the chiming guitars to the vague backing vocal twang, 'Easy To Slip' was seemingly custom-made for radio among the burgeoning country rock genre, yet its lack of a chorus combined with a tendency to ramble, didn't help its chances on the hit parade. (Producer Ted Templeman later admitted to Ben Fong-Torres: 'I think I put too much limiting on the guitars ... in retrospect, it kind of wandered around a little bit.')

Essentially forgotten almost immediately after its release (The song wasn't known to be performed live until 1992), 'Easy To Slip' was one of two early Little Feat songs ('Strawberry Flats' the other) included on the 1981 *Hoy-Hoy!* compilation. Warner Bros. once again issued the song as a single (this time backed with the original recording of Payne's 'Front Page News'), but again it went nowhere.

'Cold, Cold, Cold' (Lowell George)
With 'Easy To Slip' ostensibly serving as an album taster (a unique blend of rock and country with just a little California weirdness thrown in for good measure), any pretense to a collection of commercial radio-friendly songs with chart potential are destroyed after twelve seconds of a faint, mechanical drum pattern (provided by George's trusty Donca Matic rhythm machine), which Hayward rudely interrupts with a thunderous drum fill, clattering around his kit before settling into the syncopated rhythm. George practically howls the lyrics, actually doing so on his third introductory 'cold', his intense desperation and longing raw and primal; his future wife Liz, whom he was courting at this time despite being married to Hayward's sister-in-law Patte, later told Ben Fong-Torres in *Willin'* that she believed 'Cold, Cold, Cold' was one of three songs on the album ('Trouble' and the title track the other two) written with her in mind.

George told ZigZag in 1976 that his original demo, recorded in Hayward's living room and running over 15 minutes, served as the backing track before being transferred to the multitrack and overdubbed onto: Hayward's drums were recorded in a former meat locker at Sunset Sound Recorders, while George's harmonica (distorted to sound like a baritone sax), and, later, voice were fed to an amp placed and mic'ed in a tiled bathroom, providing its distinctive frosty sound.

The song became one of Little Feat's most popular early tracks and was a live favorite, often as a medley with 'Dixie Chicken' and 'Tripe Face Boogie.' Confirming George's penchant for tinkering with and updating older songs, 'Cold, Cold, Cold' was released as a medley with 'Tripe Face Boogie' on *Feats Don't Fail Me Now*.

'Trouble' (Lowell George)

This delicate acoustic ballad – with Payne on piano and accordion while George sings the oblique lyrics – is rife with abstract imagery – 'You yelled 'Hey' when the stove blew up/And the footprints on your ceiling are almost gone.' Yet the arrangement underlines a delicate poignancy that's close to heartbreaking: ''Cause your eyes are tired and your feet are too/And you wish the world was as tired as you.'

'Trouble' was occasionally performed live after 1992, though George's daughter Inara – a musician in her own right – covered the song frequently. She performed it in 1997 on the Lowell George tribute album *Rock and Roll Doctor*, and again in 2008 on Little Feat's *Join the Band*: fitting, as her mother – for whom the song was written – had sung it to her as a baby.

'Tripe Face Boogie' (Richie Hayward, Bill Payne)

This rare occasion of a Hayward and Payne co-write was inspired by the Houston Reception Committee: a gaggle of groupies that road manager Rick Harper arranged for Little Feat's first tour. Payne later credited the girls with not only helping him relieve his touring anxiety, but providing songwriting material. Over the next few albums, he regularly honored groupies and working girls in song.

With Hayward's unique lyric imagery – 'Buffalo'd in Buffalo, I was entertained in Houston/Yew Nork, New York, ya gotta choose one' – and Payne's boogie shuffle, the song is the perfect balance of weird and conventional. The lyrics don't make sense – which fits with the title – and they're set to a groovin' rhythm that was later adaptable to greater heights in concert. 'Tripe Face Boogie' was later coupled with 'Cold, Cold, Cold' as a medley on *Feats Don't Fail Me Now*, but in both cases the original recordings are superior. (Also worth a listen is the April 1971 demo with a false samba introduction that turns into an even more groovy arrangement.) Still, the original is superior, if only for what would become George's definitive bottleneck performance – starting low on the neck as his solo begins, in a matter of seconds stretching that

Craftsman 11/16' socket to reach the highest note, before improbably reaching an even higher one.

'Willin'' (Lowell George)

Unhappy with the debut album's version, George revisited 'Willin',' believing no song was ever truly finished. He consistently updated songs throughout his career, usually restructuring the arrangements, occasionally adding new words or simply extra instrumental embellishments. He slowed 'Willin'' down a bit, adding the full band: conjuring up a smoky, late-night truck-stop feel. While 'Sneaky' Pete Kleinow adds subtle pedal steel licks, it's Payne's sublime piano solo that steals the limelight.

One of the wisest changes was with George's vocal delivery. The earlier version sounded like he'd just taken a handful of uppers and was a little *too* eager to hit the road. Here, the pills are wearing off, and he's still got miles to go on his journey, but he'll get there, dammit. The languid pace also gives the words more room to breathe, allowing such inventive and evocative phrases as 'warped by the rain,' 'had my head stoved in,' and 'smuggled some smokes and folks from Mexico' to be appreciated, instead of being rushed by like highway billboards.

In 1976, George told *ZigZag* magazine that such vivid imagery was plucked from everyday conversation:

> I remember that I wrote it at Richie's house, where a guy was talking about the 'three wicked Ws,' which were weed, whites and wine, and I went, 'Oh, that's it.' Then Richie's sister-in-law walked into the room and said, 'Oh, look at that chair, it's been warped by the rain,' and I thought, 'I'd better start making some notes here.'

'Willin'' became George's signature song, not only for its possible contribution to his firing from The Mothers of Invention but also because he gave a voice to an otherwise unrepresented faction of Americana. In 1973, he told *Crawdaddy*, 'It's a trucker's world, so I wrote about it.' In 1978, he expanded further to *BAM*'s Mark Leviton: 'I admit I have a thing about truck drivers. After all, they're stuck like the rest of us. He might enjoy himself – the freedom of the road – but he's been through hell too.' (And just for the record, it's 585 miles from Tucson, Arizona to Tucumcari, New Mexico, and 303 miles from Tehachapi, California to Tonopah, Nevada.)

'A Apolitical Blues' (Lowell George)

Having already covered two Howlin' Wolf songs on the first album, George turns to imitation on this snarling blues rocker that pokes gentle fun at political songwriters like Bob Dylan or Pete Seeger. Instead of taking a stand, George maintains his fence-straddling, preferring not to take solicitations from the likes of Chairman Mao Zedong or John Wayne. Featuring the Beau Brummels' Ron Elliott on rhythm guitar, the track features perhaps George's nastiest bottleneck sound, while Hayward's laid-back rhythm, Payne's tinkling ivories and engineer Donn Landee's superb mix make this one of Little Feat's finest recordings.

'Sailin' Shoes' (Lowell George)
US B-side (WBS-8420), 3 August 1977

Supposedly the song that saved Little Feat at Warner Bros., George and Van Dyke Parks wrote 'Sailin' Shoes' in the studio during sessions for Parks' *Discover America*. Though George would later recall that he had most of the song written, but needed Parks' help in piecing it together. (Parks' version – included on *Discover America* to help raise George's profile – can only be described as different. Notably, both George and Hayward contributed to the album.)

Whatever the provenance, this is one of George's strangest songs – a demented blues shuffle with him again vocally imitating Howlin' Wolf (he also plays the off-beat brushed drums) and this time sliding his bottleneck across an acoustic guitar, with Payne vamping on piano and Debbie Lindsey on backing vocals. George once again weaves an oblique, abstract story; his 'cracked mosaic' songwriting approach seeping into the lyric, with imagery of a dancing 'lady in a turban, cocaine tree' blurring the song's meaning. The line about Jedidiah was a sly reference to the son of George's eventual second wife Elizabeth.

'Teenage Nervous Breakdown' (Lowell George)
One of George's oldest songs, this was first recorded by an embryonic Little Feat on 22 July 1969 as part of the demo tape for Frank Zappa's manager Herb Cohen. Another demo from later that year was released in 1981 on *Hoy-Hoy!*. In the *Hotcakes and Outtakes* liner notes, Martin Kibbee contended to Paul Barrère that the song 'went through many incarnations' before George landed on the final arrangement – a proto-punk, adrenaline-fuelled rocker with lyrics inspired by David A. Noebel's nonsensical and sensational 1966 book *Rhythm, Riots and Revolution: An Analysis of the Communist Use of Music*: which denounced the evils of rock and roll.

Though a live favorite in the band's early days, George came to dislike the song after a while and it was dropped from the setlist. But some latter-day performances absolutely smoked, with one from the Winterland Ballroom in 1976 showing up on the *Hotcakes and Outtakes* box set.

'Got No Shadow' (Bill Payne)
This is one of Payne's earliest excursions into more gospel textures, but it is a plodding mid-tempo rocker (with a hint of psychedelia) that would've suited the debut album far better. As such, it sounds positively regressive to the rest of the album. That doesn't make it a bad song, though – George sings lead and plays prominent slide guitar, with a trademark technique (lengthy sustains on one note) still in its infancy but used effectively throughout. Other arrangement touches – shakers, cowbell, a funky rhythm and dueling guitars

– hint at the direction Little Feat would soon take. They played the song live a handful of times between 1973 and 1975, but it never became a setlist staple.

'Cat Fever' (Bill Payne, Arr. Lowell George)
US B-side (WB-7553), 5 January 1972

After Payne and George met in the summer of 1969, Payne would drive up to George's house on Ben Lomond Drive and occasionally crash on the couch, though once George's wife Patte got a cat, the highly-allergic Payne crashed in George's VW van instead. (Patte later disputed this story.) Then, Charles Manson and others murdered the LaBianca family barely a mile away from Payne and the Georges. Payne later told Scoppa that afterwards, 'Although it was, like, 100 degrees ... I didn't dare open the windows, I was so freaked out.'

At least he got a good song out of it – a clearly spooked Payne created a narrative of heat-and-fever-induced paranoia:

I'll let my dogs loose
Prayin' that they will protect me
I won't let them get me
Those demon figures are after me

This was set to a George-arranged boogie rock backing, though Payne clearly relished doing his best Leon Russell impression while George perfected his bottleneck technique.

'Texas Rose Café' (Lowell George)
Originally pitched to The Doobie Brothers, this started off as an odd, strangulated blues pastiche, with George's favored rhythm syncopation and nothing even remotely approaching a melody. The lyrics were a nod to not only the aforementioned Houston Reception Committee, but also the warmer welcome the Texas fans gave the band. (Paul Barrère noted cryptically in the *Hotcakes and Outtakes* liner notes: 'All I can say, is there was always joy in Mudville when we went to Texas after that....')

The song was a suite in three sections, with a mellow, bass-dominated introduction, a military/zydeco-driven hybrid middle, and an atonal, jazz/fusion freak-out with Hayward, Payne and George pushing the boundaries – the track concluding with a reprise of the bluesy introduction, and ending vaguely with a simple cymbal crash.

Related Tracks
'Doriville' (Lowell George)
This gentle trucking song was recorded in April 1971 at the same session as the 'Tripe Face Boogie' demo, but was ultimately deemed surplus to requirements;

23

likely discarded when George opted to re-record 'Willin''. The line about rain freezing to the ground was recycled in 1973 for 'Spanish Moon.' Otherwise, the gorgeous 'Doriville' (the name a bastardization of Doraville, Georgia) languished unreleased until the 2000 *Hotcakes and Outtakes* box set.

'Roto/Tone' (Elliot Ingber)

Little Feat laid down this otherwise unrecorded Elliot Ingber composition during *Sailin' Shoes* sessions, with Ingber playing guitar so George could blow harmonica. In the *Hotcakes and Outtakes* liner notes (the recording's eventual home), Paul Barrère noted that the song 'is one of those beasts that combine boogie-woogie with (Charles) Ives; rhythm and blues with Rorschach....'

Dixie Chicken (1973)

Personnel:
Paul Barrère: guitar, vocals; co-lead vocal on 'Walkin' All Night'
Sam Clayton: congas, percussion
Lowell George: vocals, guitar; cowbell on 'Fat Man In The Bathtub'; flute on 'Juliette'
Kenny Gradney: bass
Richie Hayward: drums, vocals
Bill Payne: piano, keyboards, synthesizer, vocals; co-lead vocal on 'Walkin' All Night'
Additional personnel:
Bonnie Bramlett, Tret Fure, Gloria Jones, Debbie Lindsey, Bonnie Raitt and Stephanie Spruill: backing vocals
Danny Hutton: harmony vocal on 'Roll Um Easy'
Malcolm Cecil: synthesizer on 'Kiss It Off'
Milt Holland: tabla on 'Kiss It Off'
Fred Tackett: acoustic guitar on 'Fool Yourself'
Recorded at Clover Recorders and Sunset Sound Recorders, Los Angeles; Amigo Studios, North Hollywood, 21 October-4 December 1972
Producer: Lowell George
Release date: US: 25 January 1973
Peak position: US: -
Running time: 36:35

Unfazed by the failure of *Sailin' Shoes*, Little Feat went on tour with high hopes. They were opening for Captain Beefheart, with whom George felt more of a musical kinship than he did anyone currently on the charts, so not having a hit record wasn't his biggest concern. However, the tour was not smooth sailin', with tensions boiling to a head at Cincinnati Music Hall on 13 February 1972 – Frustrated by a non-working sound system and told it would be a two-hour fix, George decided to go ice skating, with Payne joining him: more to keep tabs on his bandmate. After 90 minutes, they returned to discover the system had been repaired in fifteen minutes. Roy Estrada was especially furious. He later quit Little Feat and joined Captain Beefheart's Magic Band, simply because Beefheart was paying a weekly wage. Hayward recalled to Bud Scoppa: '(He) made Roy an offer he couldn't refuse, like $500 a week. He left Little Feat to join Beefheart for security, which I find funnier than hell.'

George took the opportunity to expand on his musical vision and bring in some new blood. Paul Barrère was again approached to play bass, though his audition was again less than inspired. Road manager Rick Harper told Scoppa that he suggested Barrère join as rhythm guitarist:

I said, 'He's not a bass player, he's a guitar player.' So they said, 'You go get Paul, and go to your place, and you have him learn all Lowell's rhythm guitar lines.'

25

So Paul shows up and says, 'Gee man, I don't know.' I say, 'What do you mean you don't know? You can cop all these lines – you can do this shit in your sleep!'

Barrère diligently learned every line of both Little Feat albums – including some of George's leads, just in case – and, unsurprisingly, was immediately hired after nailing his audition.

But that didn't solve their original problem: they still needed a bass player. Luckily, it just so happened that Delaney and Bonnie Bramlett's marriage was breaking up, and so was their band. Bassist Kenny Gradney and conga player Sam Clayton had joined Delaney & Bonnie just at the cusp of their success – appearing on *To Bonnie from Delaney* and *Motel Shot* – but attempts at a follow-up faltered and the band splintered. Gradney was told of Little Feat's situation and contacted Payne, who invited him to his place for a meeting. Assuming he was auditioning, Gradney turned up with his bass, ready to play, but – as Gradney recalled to Scoppa – Payne stopped him:

'You don't need to audition. Rehearsal's tomorrow at noon.' But I went over to the Warner Brothers soundstage to audition anyway, and ended up jamming for five hours. Lowell just turned to me and said, 'Rehearsal's noon tomorrow. Is that OK with you?' I said, 'That's fine,' and I had the gig.

Gradney had one suggestion for George and Payne: to give his friend Sam Clayton a listen. (Sam's sister was vocalist Merry Clayton who helped give The Rolling Stones' 'Gimme Shelter' its doomed, apocalyptic atmosphere.) Gradney recalled to Ben Fong-Torres: 'I got him to come and sit with Lowell, and he loved him.' But Clayton wasn't so sure about Little Feat, as he had more lofty ambitions: 'I was trying to get with Chicago: one of the bigger bands,' he told Fong-Torres. But he'd just been offered a position with The Doobie Brothers, before it was rescinded. George extended an offer and told Clayton that time was short – the band were gearing up to go to Honolulu for the Sunshine Festival and the Crater at Diamond Head, which was all the convincing Clayton needed. Meanwhile, Gradney was impressed with his new boss, later telling Scoppa, 'I got to see Lowell work the audience. He did his job. He was awesome. It was Lowell's persona. I just knew I'd get rich with this guy. So Sam and I said the same thing: 'I'm not leaving this band.''

Infrequent live dates were peppered across the spring and summer of 1972, with the band opening for Osibisa (at the Whisky a Go Go) in May, Ramatam in July, and Stevie Wonder in June, July and August.

Sessions for the third album commenced at the end of October (Two new songs, 'Fat Man In The Bathtub' and 'Dixie Chicken,' were worked up over the live dates) and lasted six weeks. Ted Templeman hadn't returned, and there was no suggestion of asking him to. George waved it off as Templeman being 'busy making hit albums with The Doobie Brothers', though Templeman told Fong-Torres, 'I think he always wanted to be a producer more than an artist.'

George appointed himself as producer, taking the opportunity to use the studio as a blank aural canvas. But this time, he pushed himself further. In 1976, he explained:

Dixie Chicken was the first album I was really allowed to sing on, and to experiment, with microphones, etc. It's real tough, because there's always the budget hanging over your head, and that was an expensive album, but you have to live with these things for the rest of your life and it doesn't go away. You try to do your best.

But not everyone was a fan of George's methods. In 1977, Barrère was diplomatic in describing them to *Sounds* as 'making everything perfect,' and saying Hayward's drums were often recorded one at a time. Additionally, while the band recorded the backing tracks in the live room, George preferred to direct from the control booth and record his parts later. Even *he* didn't recall the sessions fondly, complaining to *Rolling Stone* in 1975 that 'The album took five years off my life.'

Despite George's ascension as producer, he no longer viewed himself as the leader, though the others assumed he *was*, simply because he wrote most of the songs. Barrère later dismissed that there was any pushback from George when it came to songwriting, telling Fong-Torres: 'Anybody who had a song, could bring it in, and we would play it, and if everybody dug it.... He was the one who really encouraged me to broaden my perspective musically, which helped immensely.' But Barrère would write only two songs with George, and that wouldn't be for another few years. Instead, Barrère and Payne developed a musical chemistry that would blossom and mature, lasting a good 40 years (give or take a few wilderness periods), with the first fruit of their labors – 'Walkin' All Night' – making it onto *Dixie Chicken*.

Dixie Chicken was released on 25 January 1973, wrapped in an unusually subtle Neon Park cover (inspired by the 'Roll Um Easy' line 'Play that concertina, I'll be your temptress'), though hardly anybody talked about it, or bought it, with only 35,000 copies sold. Bud Scoppa's *Rolling Stone* review should've shifted some units: 'We don't really need any more audacious, ingenious bands like Little Feat, we just have to support the ones that exist. I hope this band gets the support they need to stay together for a long time.'

In the meantime, they had to support themselves on the road, with a lengthy tour lasting from 11 February to 4 May. While the shows were well-attended – Bonnie Raitt was along for the ride as the opening act, and she was already a huge draw – the band had to go to extra pains to drum up promotion: which meant the now-infamous chicken suit. Barrère told Scoppa that the band were 'going to radio stations dressed as busboys and waiters, and Lowell had on the chicken suit. He wouldn't wear the head, though, so I wore the head with my busboy outfit. We were delivering boxes of Kentucky Fried Chicken that had 'Finger Pickin' Good' with the *Dixie Chicken* girl on them, as opposed to the

Colonel's face.' Already uneasy with the cheap gimmick, George discovered that this indignity wasn't helping sell records because there weren't any records to sell: local stores just weren't stocking Little Feat. Barrère told Fong-Torres, 'He got really pissed. He went and yelled and screamed at those people. He was talking about calling the whole thing off at that point.'

Another tour followed in the summer and autumn, but frustrations continued to mount, culminating in George firing Hayward in November, replacing him with Freddie White: brother of Earth, Wind & Fire's Maurice and Verdine. George told Andy Childs in *ZigZag* that the band broke up 'for about two days. I think I called Bill on the phone and called him a son of a bitch and said 'fuck you' and hung up.' They regrouped, of course, but *Dixie Chicken* could very well have been their epitaph. All it took to save Little Feat, was a temporary relocation to Maryland.

'Dixie Chicken' (Lowell George, Martin Kibbee)
US A-side (WB-7689), March 1973; UK A-side (K-16524), March 1975

The third album's title track dated back to the second album when George and Martin Kibbee were writing *that* title track. An exhausted Kibbee had left Little Feat's rehearsal space in Laurel Canyon at two in the morning, when he passed an all-night restaurant promoting 'dixie chicken.' Haunted by an incessant riff George had come up with just before leaving, Kibbee had the song written by the time he got home. He told Bud Scoppa: 'I showed up the next day. They were rehearsing on the soundstage at Warner Brothers that day. Lowell read it and said, 'You fuckin' nut. No way.''

Kibbee wrote the words, and George brought them to life: casting himself as a hapless drunk who falls victim to a temptress's wiles. The two hit the nightlife – 'My money flowed like wine' – one thing leads to another, and he finds himself living the American dream with his Tennessee lamb. Of course, there's no such thing as a happy ending, and before long, he's lonely and at the bar of the Commodore Hotel again. Unable to get her off his mind, he finds a sympathetic ear in the bartender 'who said he knew her well.' As it turns out, so do the other gentlemen in the bar.

Set to George's laid-back, gently-funky groove – which Hayward, Gradney and Clayton ease into quickly – 'Dixie Chicken' comfortably announces the new-look Little Feat without going *too* extreme (George saved the more adventurous stuff for later). George snakes his bottleneck guitar between Payne's barrelhouse piano and the tenacious groove. Barrère adds a few fills here and there but mostly doubles Gradney, while a six-strong backing vocal group (most of whom became accomplished solo acts in their own right) sweeten the choruses.

Released in March 1973 – shortly after the album release – as a single b/w 'Lafayette Railroad,' 'Dixie Chicken' failed to chart. Two years later, the song was released as Little Feat's debut UK single, with 'Oh Atlanta' on the flipside. But despite strong word-of-mouth and an appearance as part of the Warners

Bros. Music Show (with fellow labelmates The Doobie Brothers and Tower of Power), the single again failed to chart.

The song became a live favorite, often as the second song in a medley bookended by 'Cold, Cold, Cold' and 'Tripe Face Boogie,' and later as the song itself. In keeping with Little Feat's improvisational nature, 'Dixie Chicken' would often be a launching pad for the band to go off into unchartered territory, and, on more than one occasion, a guitar lick or drum groove would evolve into a fully-formed song. It's also one of the band's most-played live songs, with nearly 2,500 performances documented.

'Two Trains' (Lowell George)
One of George's most accomplished compositions, this has stellar production and a flawless performance. Opening with relaxed interplay between Payne's electric piano, Barrère's wah-wah guitar and Gradney's bass, it gains steam with Clayton's congas and George's slide, with considerable added sustain giving the impression of a wailing train whistle, before Hayward rudely interrupts with a fill to settle the band into a laid-back funk groove.

The song is largely autobiographical, but it doesn't matter whether the love George is singing about is music, a woman, or just a friend – he's a conflicted man, and would rather leave the decision-making to someone else: 'You know it would be alright, be just fine/If the woman took one train and left the other behind.'

George demoed the song in the *Sailin' Shoes* sessions, with a completely different lyric and vocal/guitar arrangement and a primitive Korg rhythm machine: the Donca Matic. Later in the decade, he updated the song with new lyrics and an even funkier arrangement for his 1979 solo album *Thanks, I'll Eat It Here*.

'Roll Um Easy' (Lowell George)
Dixie Chicken settles in with this near-solo George performance, more in line with the first album's late-night truck-stop weepers. By far the most accomplished song George had written to date, 'Roll Um Easy' is a simple love song, similar to 'Willin'', with George wearing his heart on his sleeve: 'Oh I am just a vagabond/A drifter on the run.' But even a rock and roll outlaw can find love: 'And baby I'm defenceless/Singin' harmony, in unison/Sweet harmony/Gotta hoist your flag and I'll beat your drum.'

Three Dog Night's Danny Hutton stopped by Clover Recorders to visit George but was quickly drafted in to sing the harmony vocal. He told Scoppa: 'I'd just come back from touring, and my voice was really kind of burned out. I did it once, and it sounded terrible. (George) said, 'That was great. You sound awful, it's wonderful.' And that was it, one take. I sound like a rough old man on that track. He really knew what he wanted.'

Always keen on evolving his own songs and never believing a song was too precious or beyond an update, George drastically retooled and re-recorded 'Roll Um Easy' for his 1979 solo album *Thanks, I'll Eat It Here*, giving it a more

lively feel. Recorded between 26 October and 9 November 1976 at Sunset
Sound Recorders, that arrangement strips away the original's ragged weariness
in favor of a more soulful – if conventional – performance. Ultimately it was
deemed surplus to requirements, remaining unreleased until the *Hotcakes
and Outtakes* box set: which credits Little Feat with the performance, though
Barrère didn't recall playing on it.

'On Your Way Down' (Allen Toussaint)
Despite being one of the most influential songwriters of the 1950s and 1960s,
Allen Toussaint didn't release his first album (not counting 1958's *The Wild
Sounds of New Orleans*: credited pseudonymously to Tousan) until 1971's
superb *Toussaint*. But it was the following year's *Life, Love and Faith* that earned
widespread praise – from those who knew about it (It seems Toussaint also
suffered record company distribution and promotion issues). Lowell George was
a longtime Toussaint fan, and deeming 'On Your Way Down' worthy of covering
on the new album, immediately adapted it to Little Feat's new sound.

Opening with Payne's majestic grand-piano flourishes, the song eases into its
simmering groove, George taking his time getting to the first verse, allowing
the band to cook up the tension. This isn't a happy song – Toussaint openly
celebrating the downfall of a prominent person who has long abused others
while making his way to the top, which makes George's sweet-as-honey vocal
all the more effective ('You think it's an honor just to have you around').
George made a few instrumental tweaks – Toussaint's horns and harmonica
replaced with bottleneck guitar and backing vocalists – but the performance
otherwise remains largely faithful to the original.

The song was a steady presence in the setlist, with over 300 performances
from its debut at Paul's Mall in Boston on 1 April 1973, to its two by-then-rare
appearances in 2018.

'Kiss It Off' (Lowell George)
This unintentional companion piece to 'On Your Way Down' is more a studio
experiment than an actual song. George eschews conventional instrumentation
for synthesizer (played by Payne and Malcolm Cecil) and tabla (Milt Holland)
– conjuring up a menacing, sinister atmosphere. Going by the title alone,
George is obviously displeased with someone, but the oblique lyric imagery
('some electric nightmare,' 'the swords of fire,' 'on the hopes of a tyrant')
makes it inscrutable. With its spacey instrumentation (The synthesizer bleeps
and bloops swirling in stereo no doubt elicited cries of stoned astonishment),
plodding arrangement and strained vocal, 'Kiss It Off' is best viewed as a
gimmick than a serious performance.

'Fool Yourself' (Fred Tackett)
Fred Tackett first met Lowell at a party at songwriter Jimmy Webb's house in the
late 1960s, and had stayed in regular contact ever since. Tackett moved to Los

Angeles and found work as a session musician, but he was also a songwriter, with one song, in particular, finding favor with George. Lowell heard Tackett's 'Fool Yourself' and said, 'I'm gonna record that one.'

George wasn't just blowing smoke: Little Feat recorded it for *Dixie Chicken*, and Tackett was invited to play acoustic guitar. While at the studio, Tackett noticed the caliber of the musicians George had recruited for the sessions, and established the Feats Auxiliary: a nebulous and ever-evolving group of friends who would contribute to each other's endeavors. Tackett later told Scoppa: 'There were all kinds of friends coming in doing one little thing with the band, like Tret Fure, Bonnie Raitt and Emmylou Harris.' Other musicians who floated in the periphery included Three Dog Night's Danny Hutton, Bonnie Bramlett, and Gloria Jones. Others – like Emmylou Harris, Linda Ronstadt and Michael McDonald – followed on subsequent albums.

Unusually – despite Tackett joining Little Feat full-time in 1988 – they didn't play this song live until 1992, with only 22 performances since.

'Walkin' All Night' (Paul Barrère, Bill Payne)

Set to a rollicking boogie rhythm, this inaugural Payne/Barrère co-write is more loose than the rest of *Dixie Chicken*, with George letting loose on bottleneck, while Payne and Barrère trade lyric lines of searching for the right prostitute. The band is clearly having a ball here (augmented on the choruses by almost everyone who showed up to the session that day), and while the lyric might've been a little blue for the hit parade, it captured the spirit of its songwriters perfectly, serving as the perfect launching pad for their working partnership.

'Walkin' All Night' was an immediate live favorite – often played between 1973 and 1978, usually as the concert opener. Subsequent appearances were fewer and farther between, though it still pops up every now and then, much to the audience's delight.

'Fat Man In The Bathtub' (Lowell George)

If ever there was a perfect summation of Lowell George in a four-minute pop song, this is it – and not because of his then-increasing and widening frame. His sense of humor and mischief are on full display here – from the tongue-in-cheek lyrics about Spotcheck Billy and his sweet taquita Juanita, to the unconventional rhythm: a product of George's fascination with odd time signatures and his liberal use of a razor blade to tape.

George's demo – released in 2002 on *Raw Tomatos, Volume One* – was the best song The Rolling Stones never recorded, with George marrying a gritty Keith-Richards-like riff to a sneering Jagger-esque vocal, over a chugging Donca Matic pattern. On the album, it had transformed into a laid-back boogie rocker, with moaning backing vocals and a hiccuping drum pattern. A pleased Hayward told *Modern Drummer* that songs like 'Fat Man' were 'important stepping stones in my growth because I got to learn different ways to play 4/4 time; different ways to enjoy a backbeat. 'Fat Man' was one of my first

31

experiments in second line. It began with that straight Bo Diddley thing you hear in the intro, and through the course of the tune, it changes feels about six times. They're all at the same tempo, but they feel completely different.'

The song became a live favorite, with nearly 2,000 documented performances (their third most-performed track after 'Willin'' and 'Dixie Chicken'), and an especially stellar version opened their 1978 live album *Waiting for Columbus*. They also played the song on *The Old Grey Whistle Test* (along with 'Rock and Roll Doctor') – a version notable for George's sleepy appearance and lethargic vocal: not the result of excess, but because some bright spark decided that 9:00 a.m. was the perfect time to film it.

'Juliette' (Lowell George)
First recorded by the original Little Feat on 22 July 1969 at T.T.G. (first released on *Lightning-Rod Man*: an unusual compilation of pre-Little-Feat recordings; later on *Hotcakes and Outtakes*), 'Juliette' was dusted off and updated for *Dixie Chicken*; changed from an upbeat rocker to a more soulful, slow lament. Despite George's flute-playing – which is more distracting than interesting – the track is superb, with the lighter, jazz-like arrangement serving it well.

Largely forgotten, 'Juliette' was brought out of mothballs for eight live performances in 1975 and 1976, often in conjunction with 'Lafayette Railroad.'

'Lafayette Railroad' (Lowell George, Bill Payne)
US B-side (WB-7689), March 1973

Dixie Chicken closes with this rather lethargic groove piece, co-written by George and Payne but offering neither a chance to show off their respective chops. George's bottleneck guitar is rather rote, while Payne sticks to the incessant riff. At least Hayward comes to life in the outro, breaking the monotonous pattern with some trademark flourishes: but by then, the song is fading out.

Related Tracks
'Ace In The Hole' (Paul Barrère)
Barrère wasted no time in submitting his first song to Little Feat. But this semi-autobiographical country/boogie rocker was ultimately deemed surplus to requirements. Retooled as 'High Roller' in 1975 for *The Last Record Album*, the song was again rejected before another (slight) title change and arrangement tweak rendered it releasable as the opener for 1977's *Time Loves a Hero*.

'Eldorado Slim' (Bill Payne, Lowell George)
This live favorite was cooked up onstage in Little Feat's first incarnation and was regularly used as an improvisational launching pad. In the *Hotcakes and Outtakes* liner notes, Barrère recalled, 'This was one of the first songs

we learned when Kenny, Sam and I joined the band.' By the time the second incarnation was playing the song, it had turned into a barnstormer, which made its somewhat sterile studio performance all the more disappointing – perhaps because of the omission of George's usual risqué preamble about the titular character picking up a hitchhiking 'hippie chick in a red velvet jumpsuit with tomatoes': George's typical absurdist sense of humor setting the scene perfectly. Or perhaps sometimes what is normally a live instrumental jam just doesn't translate well to the studio.

'Airplane,' 'Chevy '39,' 'Bag Of Reds,' 'Ass For Days'

These four titles were early live jams, cooked up (like 'Eldorado Slim') onstage, this time after Gradney, Clayton and Barrère had joined the band. 'Airplane' and 'Chevy '39' didn't survive setlists beyond 1973, while 'Bag Of Reds' – a barbiturate-inspired pastiche of 'Duke Of Earl,' stuck around as late as 1975. Only 'Ass For Days' – a lascivious blues parody that left little to the imagination – survived as late as 1978, with a live recording of indeterminate origin (Barrère estimated at being from either 1974 or 1975) ending up on *Raw Tomatos Vol. 1*.

Feats Don't Fail Me Now (1974)

Personnel:
Paul Barrère: guitar, vocals; lead vocal on 'Skin It Back'
Sam Clayton: percussion, vocals
Lowell George: vocals, guitar
Kenny Gradney: bass
Richie Hayward: drums, vocals
Bill Payne: keyboards, vocals; lead vocal on 'Oh Atlanta'
Additional personnel:
Gordon DeWitty: clavinet on 'Spanish Moon'
Fred White: drums on 'Spanish Moon'
Tower of Power (Greg Adams: trumpet/arrangement; Mic Gillette: trumpet, trombone; Lenny Pickett: alto sax; Emilio Castillo: tenor sax; Steve 'Doc' Kipka: baritone sax): horns on 'Spanish Moon'
Emmylou Harris, Bonnie Raitt and Fran Tate: backing vocals
Recorded at Blue Seas Recording Studio, Hunt Valley, June 1974; except 'Spanish Moon' recorded at Sunset Sound and the Sound Factory, Los Angeles, and Amigo Studios, North Hollywood, 25 January-30 March 1974
Producer: Lowell George; 'Spanish Moon' produced by Van Dyke Parks.
Release date: US: 9 August 1974
Peak position: US: 36
Running time: 34:25

Barrère told Bud Scoppa: 'You could say that *Feats Don't Fail Me Now* was a literal title, because Lowell got us all back together again and said, 'Okay, we're gonna sink or swim with this one.''

Little Feat had put all their renewed energy behind *Dixie Chicken*, but its dispiriting sales and even more dispiriting tour had driven George to break up the band, temporarily. More a hiatus than an actual disbandment, the time was spent wisely, with the individual musicians finding lucrative session work. While George secured most of that work (with Payne a not-too-distant second, even turning down an offer to join The Doobie Brothers), to his credit he invited members of Little Feat along whenever possible – John Cale's *Paris 1919* featured Payne and Hayward; Kathy Dalton's *Amazing* included all of Little Feat; Chico Hamilton's *Chico the Master* had all Little Feat members except Hayward, and Bonnie Raitt's *Takin' My Time* featured Payne and Barrère.

But before long, George was compelled to reunite Little Feat (Hayward was still *persona non grata*, having been dismissed in November 1973) and make good on his promise to co-produce the new Feats album with Van Dyke Parks, with sessions in late January as the trial run. But there were problems immediately. George remembered, 'We got into an enormous argument with Warner Bros. because Van Dyke is famous for his huge budgets. He was going to do more, but we reached a point where we got stuck, and the band broke up.'

They still got a few tracks recorded in Los Angeles – an embryonic 'Feats Don't Fail Me Now' and 'Brickyard Blues' – but Parks focused on 'Spanish Moon': eventually the only track released from those sessions. Parks later told Bud Scoppa:

> We met Tower of Power, who came down from San Francisco – a group that was sizzling at the time at Warner Bros. It was just natural that they should do it. Lowell looked at me and asked, 'What does a producer do?' A producer gets food at 2:00 a.m., which is what I did. The session went very well.

Except George still wasn't convinced that Little Feat had a future, telling *ZigZag* in 1975: 'It was a great hobby, but we weren't making any money. We really weren't surviving. So I suggested to everybody that we try and find employment while we figure out a new hustle.' He readily accepted British rock and soul singer Robert Palmer's offer to record with him in New Orleans. (A decade before Palmer's made-for-MTV polished corporate look, he was working on his debut album *Sneakin' Sally Through the Alley* with New Orleans' The Meters as his rhythm section.) George told *ZigZag* that while he was there, Feat's manager Bob Cavallo contacted him about International Telecom Incorporated – a recording studio in Hunt Valley: a suburb not too far from Baltimore, Maryland: 'And I dropped everything and said, 'Yikes, that's it!'.'

Former Lovin' Spoonful bassist Steve Boone purchased the location, named it Blue Seas, and offered Little Feat cheap studio time. Barrère told Ben Fong-Torres: 'We got this studio for five thousand a month, locked out. So, for fifteen thousand, we had a zillion hours.' The Blue Seas house engineer George Massenburg had met Lowell at a Mike Auldridge session and quickly became a sympathetic ear – and later to Payne and Barrère – and an integral player in Little Feat's sound. But Massenburg told Bud Scoppa the first recording day was 'utterly unmemorable. 'Transactional' is the best word. As musicians, they were competent beyond what I had been used to either in the US or Europe. Bill was an amazing keyboardist. But I suppose the thing that stood out is how cool Lowell, Bill and Paul were.'

But according to Barrère, Maryland meant more than a cheap recording studio and some new blood:

> We really got hooked into the Washington, D.C. scene. It was like our home away from home. People embraced us as if we were a local band, just from the three months we'd spent there recording. It was amazing. We could go to Washington and sell lots of tickets. We also played a bunch of the small colleges in the region … Obviously, we have a lot of memories about the Baltimore/Washington area.

There was also a spirit of domesticity and matrimony at the time: At Blue Seas, Payne met engineer/singer Fran Tate (the album backing singer with Bonnie

Raitt and Emmylou Harris) and they start dating, eventually marrying in 1977; Barrère met Towson native Debbie Donovan, also eventually marrying, though only briefly, as – according to Barrère – Los Angeles and the Little Feat world overwhelmed Donovan, and the marriage ended two years later. Lowell's wife Liz gave birth to a daughter – Inara – on 4 July: six weeks after the cross-country move from Hollywood to their rented home in Cockeysville. Liz told Fong-Torres: 'Just getting away was great because it was really touch and go at that point. Hollywood was getting to be not a very good influence, and so it was wonderful they all went to *the country*. Everybody had a good time.' Payne agreed, telling Mary Turner in 1984: 'It was the best time of my life … It felt more like a band.'

In 1976, George described *Feats Don't Fail Me Now* (released on the day of President Nixon's resignation) as a 'party record – have a beer or two and dance … that's the frame of mind we were in for that record.' *Rolling Stone*'s Ben Gerson agreed, but only after begrudging the band's evolution:

Little Feat began as a writer's band, the writers being keyboardist Bill Payne and slide guitarist/singer Lowell George. By the group's second album *Sailin' Shoes*, George's voice and guitar had progressed to the point where Little Feat was no longer just a writer's band – material, performance and production were held in equipoise through that album and its successor *Dixie Chicken*. On *Feats Don't Fail Me Now*, that perfect tension has slackened … the songs on Feats – though within the group's chosen speciality – do not evoke the frenzy of their counterparts on *Dixie Chicken*: like 'Two Trains' and 'Fat Man In The Bathtub.' The syncopations of 'Rock And Roll Doctor' are riveting, but the tune's overall format is too choppy to be uplifting. Yet, along with the title song, 'Down The Road' and guitarist Paul Barrère's 'Skin It Back,' it qualifies as fine dance music.

Noel Coppage wrote in *Stereo Review*: 'The Feat are good lick-hitters, but generally play it tight. The lyrics – what one can catch of them – are a gas; the main problem is that the tunes are thin. Rock is famous for that, of course, and this band compensates nicely by being dead-on with the rhythms.'

Billboard were effusive with their praise, though, confusingly, they name-checked two songs that didn't even appear on the album: 'The band is excellent, potentially commercial, and it's a real mystery why they have not made it to a larger extent than they have. The band must rank near the top of any meaningful list of today's groups. Best cuts: 'Rock And Roll Doctor', 'Long Distance Love,' 'Front Page News,' 'Feats Don't Fail Me Now'.' (An early printing of the rear sleeve had a completely different tracklist – 'Rock And Roll Doctor', 'Oh Atlanta', 'Long Distance Love' and 'Front Page News' made up side one, while side two had the title track, 'The Fan', 'Skin It Back' and the *Sailin' Shoes* medley. The record itself played the *Feats* album correctly. Perhaps *Billboard* received an early pressing(?))

Billboard's point about Little Feat's success would prove to be prophetic – All the hard work had paid off, and whether it was the music, the eccentric Neon Park cover of Marilyn Monroe and George Washington in a Lincoln speeding away from a crackle of lightning, or the band's reputation, *Feats Don't Fail Me Now* was a hit, peaking at 36 in the US and selling 150,000 copies within a few months, eventually hitting half a million and going gold. George was pleased, telling *Rolling Stone* at the end of the year: 'Now we're a third-rate *known* band. Maybe even second-rate. And I think now's the right time to go to Europe.'

And so they did, joining the Warner Bros. Music Show: a two-pronged package tour that paired up three bands each and sent them across Europe with label executives, publicists, road managers and crew (Over 100 people in total). Little Feat was teamed up with The Doobie Brothers and Tower of Power (The other group package consisted of Graham Central Station, Montrose and Bonaroo), and started their three-week jaunt in Manchester on 15 January 1975.

The Doobies were generally the headliners, but that changed four days later at London's Rainbow Theatre, with *ZigZag*'s Andy Childs reporting that 'It was refreshingly apparent to note that the overwhelming majority of people had primarily come to see Little Feat, and I can't imagine that anyone left the Rainbow that evening without the feeling that they'd seen one of the best bands in the world ... they were just magic.' The audience agreed, and when the Doobies followed Little Feat shortly after, a good portion of the crowd had dispersed.

To their credit, Little Feat weren't trying to one-up anybody, though Barrère noted that the headline of an unnamed British paper – 'Trampled by Little Feat' – 'made it very hard for the rest of the tour.' Childs 'genuinely felt sorry for the Doobies, who clearly found it impossible to follow them, and ended up playing as meekly and politely as they could,' though the Doobies were about to recruit Michael McDonald and achieve success Little Feat could only dream of.

As for Little Feat, they thrived on the vibe and flourished in their foreign surroundings, with friendships and musical kinship formed along the way, all while maintaining an approachable air: at the end of an interview with Childs, George thanked him for asking such interesting questions.

Warner Bros. tried to capitalize on the success by releasing 'Dixie Chicken' (b/w 'Oh Atlanta') as a single that March, but the tour had ended by that point and the single didn't sell. (Far more effective was the band's appearance on *The Old Grey Whistle Test*, where they played 'Rock And Roll Doctor' and 'Fat Man In The Bathtub,' at the decidedly un-rock-and-roll hour of 9:00 a.m.) But Warners had laid the groundwork – the British and mainland European audiences loved Little Feat, and each successive album would expand on the sales of its predecessor, even earning the band some much-needed chart action. The Feats, it seemed, hadn't failed.

'Rock And Roll Doctor' (Lowell George, Martin Kibbee)

'I use tape like someone would use manuscript paper,' George told *ZigZag* magazine in 1975, and this is a perfect example. Stuck with a bunch of different musical ideas on separate pieces of tape, he combined them all into one and presented the result to Payne, who then had the unenviable task of making sense of it. Co-writer Martin Kibbee explained in the *Hoy-Hoy!* liner notes:

> Lowell was determined to make 'Rock And Roll Doctor' musically complicated, which made it a quite difficult process. Most songs are written in a quite straightforward fashion, you know: A, B, C section, chorus, bridge. But Lowell used to talk in terms of the 'cracked mosaic' ... and I think that song is a prime example of intentional irregularity.

As a result of its strange journey (Chorus one has an extra bar of rest; a guitar solo follows verse two instead of another chorus, which ultimately ends the song), 'Rock And Roll Doctor' was malleable in a way that other Feats songs were not, meaning it could be embellished upon or stretched out with relative ease. For a case of the former, listen to the *Hoy-Hoy!* version, which adds an Allen-Toussaint-arranged horn section; for the latter, check out the version on *Live In Holland 1976,* which absolutely simmers.

'Oh Atlanta' (Bill Payne)

US A-side (WBS-8054), 6 November 1974; UK B-side (K-16524), March 1975

While Payne and George were infrequently credited as collaborators, they did challenge each other as songwriters. Payne recalled to Ben Fong-Torres:

> Lowell would say, 'You can't write a commercial song,' And I'd say, 'Yeah, I can.' My idea of a hit record then was basically something with a chorus coming in at around 45 seconds. The result was 'Oh Atlanta.' It wasn't a hit record, but it was one of those songs that's stood the test of time.

Inspired by the midwestern pastime of watching planes take off and land, Payne told Bud Scoppa that he wrote 'a semi-poem about people watching planes take off and birds on a wire. Then I met this redhead girl in Atlanta: Sherry. Several years later, I married those images of being in a place where you're down near Ohio at the airport, watching people taking off on planes, wishing I was on one to Atlanta. It was a real visual song.'

Set to a rollicking boogie backing that's not quite hellbound, the song still has a commercial appeal that other Feats songs lacked – indeed, its non-performance as a chart single is baffling, but it did become an immediate live favorite, and was performed – albeit in truncated form – on German TV's *Musikladen*. George especially excelled in his slide guitar obligations, and later lavished praise on the song, in his own way. He told Bill Flanagan: 'One time I said, 'Bill, these songs you're writing.' I was real blunt with him one time. And right after that, he came up with 'Oh Atlanta,' which to me is a very successful song.'

'Skin It Back' (Paul Barrère)
Barrère's first-released song for Little Feat is one of his most celebrated – its origins rooted in the promotional disillusionment that soured the tour for *Dixie Chicken.*

In the *Hoy-Hoy!* liner notes, Barrère recalled that this particular period was 'strange, funny, and degrading,' but at least he got a classic song out of it. It became a live favorite, often as part of a medley with 'Spanish Moon' and 'Fat Man In The Bathtub', though occasionally it opened a concert – such a versatile song it was.

'Down The Road' (Lowell George)
US B-side (WBS-8054), 6 November 1974; US B-side (WBS-8091), 26 March 1975

Perhaps the album's least-celebrated song, this is a showcase for George's bottleneck abilities, with a particularly skillful, double-tracked feature more than halfway through. Once again he's in the mood for some hit and run:

> You say faster so I speed up
> But still I'm much too slow
> I feel your innuendo
>
> Come over here and try to get me off
> Won't you please me
> Shake your dignity

But the story goes nowhere and the lyrics fall flat, with even George sounding unconvinced.

'Spanish Moon' (Lowell George)
US A-side (WBS-8091), 26 March 1975

Side one closes with this atmospheric funk piece, cooked up by George in a jam session at the band's new Burbank rehearsal space. Clayton told Fong-Torres: 'I just started doing this beat, and Lowell came in and said, 'Just hold that, and do *this*.' And he showed Kenny a bass line, and he said, 'I've got this song.' And he started doing this thing, and that's how we got it.'

Released in March 1975 as the album's second single, 'Spanish Moon' unsurprisingly failed to chart; the lines about whiskey and bad cocaine deemed too *risqué* for radio and appropriately excised. But the song became a live favorite, often kicking off a medley including 'Skin It Back' and 'Fat Man In The

39

Bathtub', though 'Spanish Moon' would later be performed in its own right. After George's death, Clayton sang it in concert, with a version recorded with Pure Prairie League singer Craig Fuller released on the 2008 Little Feat album *Join the Band*.

'Feats Don't Fail Me Now' (Paul Barrère, Lowell George, Martin Kibbee)

This joyous, ebullient title track was the first Barrère/George collaboration (with help from Kibbee), though its origins were a point of dispute in the *Hotcakes and Outtakes* box set, with Kibbee insisting he'd scribbled the lyrics on a cocktail napkin, handed them to George, and never heard another word about it; Barrère insisted he heard the phrase in an Abbott and Costello movie he'd watched the night before and remembered in his overindulged fog. Barrère wrote in *Hotcakes*: 'Either Mantan Moreland or Stepin Fetchit was in it, and at one particularly scary moment, the line was delivered.'

Whatever its origins, the song is one of the band's finest, filled again with trucker imagery ('Don't the sunrise look so pretty, never such a sight/Like a-rollin' into New York City/With the skyline in the morning light') and sexual innuendo ('Heard you got the biggest, hmm, the biggest truck in town') reflecting George and Barrère's humor. The performance is a blast, with Payne especially shining on piano (George matches him at times on slide guitar). Live, the song would be extended beyond its two-and-a-half-minute length, with George grabbing the microphone and leading the crowd in a call-and-response. Each band member would then leave their instrument and wave goodnight, with only bassist Gradney keeping the groove going, before the band returned, finishing with a show-stopping grand finale.

'The Fan' (Lowell George, Bill Payne)

One of the oldest songs in the Little Feat catalog, this early George/Payne co-write was first recorded in the debut album sessions. Payne told Barrère in the *Hotcakes* liner notes:

> I remember being down at a rehearsal studio on La Cienega Blvd, and here's Linda Ronstadt sleeping on the floor, and Jackson Browne's there running around, and I have two keyboards set up so I can play one with the left hand and one with the right, and I come up with this lick ... Lowell digs the groove and writes some lyrics along the lines of cheerleaders-gone-bad, and *boom*: a song is born.

But, like several other early songs, George decided it needed time to marinate and returned to it for *Feats*. By this time, the song had been in regular setlist rotation, so they had a more robust arrangement mapped out, making it relatively quick to record. Hayward was especially proud of his performance, telling *Modern Drummer* in October 1995: 'That was probably the most difficult thing I've ever done ... One of the challenging aspects of the song was playing the fast 7/8 feel and improvising on it under the solo. There's one phrase in 10 and a couple in what sounds like 8, but it's really 16 chopped up into different segments. It got real interesting.'

'Medley: Cold, Cold, Cold/Tripe Face Boogie' (Lowell George, Richie Hayward, Bill Payne)

The album ends on a weak note, with an updated medley of two *Sailin' Shoes* tracks, similar to how they were performed live (or not: 'Dixie Chicken' was almost always sandwiched in between). The performance is fine enough, but the claustrophobic chill of the original 'Cold, Cold, Cold' is gone completely; 'Tripe Face Boogie' is given a jazz-fusion keyboard solo, but is otherwise unchanged from the original. Considering some of the known album outtakes ('Brickyard Blues,' 'Long Distance Love,' 'Front Page News'), the decision to fill up ten minutes of precious vinyl with two previously-released songs was kind of a rip-off.

Related Tracks
'Brickyard Blues' (Allen Toussaint)

Recorded at the same sessions as 'Spanish Moon' and an embryonic 'Feats Don't Fail Me Now', this Allen Toussaint cover benefits from George's soulful vocal and Payne's tasty piano. But it's the Tower of Power horn section that brings it home. Why it languished unreleased until 2000's *Hotcakes and Outtakes,* is a mystery, as *Feats* would have benefited greatly from its inclusion.

The Last Record Album (1975)

Personnel:
Paul Barrère: guitar, vocals; co-lead vocal on 'Romance Dance' and 'Day Or Night'
Sam Clayton: congas, vocals
Lowell George: vocals, guitar
Kenny Gradney: bass
Richie Hayward: drums, vocals
Bill Payne: keyboards, synthesizer, vocals; co-lead vocal on 'Romance Dance' and 'Day Or Night'; lead vocal on 'Somebody's Leavin''
Additional personnel:
John Hall: guitar on 'All That You Dream'
Valerie Carter and Fran Tate: backing vocals on 'Long Distance Love' and 'One Love Stand'
Recorded at the Sound Factory, Hollywood, March-September 1975
Producer: Lowell George
Release date: US: 17 October 1975
Peak position: US: 36, UK: 36
Running time: 34:13

'The real name of this record is *The First Record Album*,' wrote Lowell George in what had now become his customary stream-of-consciousness liner notes, for Little Feat's fifth album ('So let no paranoia ensue,' he added, to ward off any accusations that the band was breaking up). While that may have been a name better reserved for *Dixie Chicken*, there's no denying that this album marks a transition – George finally abdicated his role as Little Feat's ultimate leader, as his friend Martin Kibbee had feared he would become.

Payne later recognised this dynamic band shift, in the *Hotcakes and Outtakes* liner notes:

I just felt somewhat dismissed with my own material, in some cases. It felt so chaotic. I'd also been doing a shitload of sessions over the years with The Doobie Brothers, Bonnie, Jackson and a lot of others, and I knew that not every session you walked into would be half as insane as ours were. Why does it have to be so adversarial? And you know, I was contributing to that because of my personality, not to lay it all on Lowell, which I was doing at the time. The truth is, it was part of what we were.

Frustrated that he could no longer count on George as a collaborator, Payne found a sympathetic ear in Barrère, whose Little Feat songwriting had so far been minimal but mighty. ('Skin It Back' – Barrère's first solo composition – became a live favorite, while his co-write with Payne on 'Walkin' All Night' and with George and Kibbee on 'Feats Don't Fail Me Now,' were important.) Payne and Barrère co-wrote the album's standout track 'All That You Dream' (rescued from the *Feats* sessions), with assistance from Kenny Gradney on 'Romance Dance' and

'One Love Stand.' 'Hi Roller' – Barrère's only solo contribution – was brought out of mothballs from the *Dixie Chicken* sessions (when it had been known as 'Ace In The Hole'), and nearly made the cut, with the lyrics printed on the sleeve – George crossed these out with black sharpie, scrawling an apologetic 'Maybe next time' over them. (Indeed, the song opened the next album.)

George's contributions were scarce but stellar: 'Long Distance Love' – another 'Maybe next time' from the *Feats* sessions – is the obvious highlight, and earned wider exposure when the band was filmed recording it at their rehearsal space The Alley for *The Old Grey Whistle Test*, with 'Whispering' Bob Harris once again heaping praise on the band. 'Down Below The Borderline' recalls the early raw Little Feat. Only 'Mercenary Territory' was a co-write – with Hayward, though George's widow Elizabeth (given a belated co-credit on *Hotcakes*) claimed it was simply because of Hayward's drum fills.

Payne rounded out the record with the quirky Steely-Dan-inspired 'Day Or Night' and the sublime 'Somebody's Leavin'' – the latter written (and performed only once) during the brief seven-month period when Fred White replaced Hayward. By that count, the playing field for the songwriters is relatively even, with Payne and Barrère (and Gradney) obviously more willing to collaborate than George at that point.

Yet the album can't escape its reputation as Barrère and Payne's jazz-fusion *coup d'état*, with George the helpless victim. Indeed, shortly before his death, he played up the injured-party angle in interviews, which soured some former supporters in the music press when Little Feat reformed in the 1980s. But George was, in fact, the instigator. He told *ZigZag* in August 1976:

I wish for everyone in the band to step forward. For a long time, I was getting a lot of attention, but, for example, Bill Payne is a magnificent musician and also deserves a lot of attention. Basically, the idea ... is that we should all do our best and have a good time. If it doesn't happen, that's the breaks, and if it does, great.

It's not surprising that George sounded so calculated and deliberate (Earlier in 1975, he diplomatically told *Streetlife* in relation to the new album: 'I felt it was time that Bill made his statement, and I left him all the room I could.'). His attention had shifted from Little Feat to other hobbies and interests: mainly fatherhood. Barrère later explained: 'He had a daughter and didn't like going on the road, so he relinquished a lot of things to us. It was a strange time.'

Clayton was perhaps the bluntest in his assessment of the alleged coup: 'It wasn't like they (Barrère and Payne) had more say, it was just like Lowell sort of withdrew. He wouldn't have new material. He had material and stuff, but he was saying, 'Let these guys go and do this,' And he just let them do more stuff.'

So there was no mutiny. Payne and Barrère simply recognized that someone needed to steer the ship, and George wasn't up to the task. Besides, the band's status was rising and they were getting noticed – Mick Jagger, Jimmy Page and

Bob Dylan were frequent concert guests, and Robert Plant lamented on *The Old Grey Whistle Test* that Little Feat deserved more recognition.

The pressure was now on to deliver an album that would generate more sales. While their albums had never been big sellers, *Feats* had broken the 200,000 mark. And with a prime position in the Warners Bros. Music Show, the label was finally putting the weight of their promotions department behind the band. As a result, *The Last Record Album* sold over 300,000 copies and – most impressively – spent three weeks in the UK chart, ultimately matching their US position of 36.

Reviews were complimentary, for the most part. The *Village Voice*'s Robert Christgau called the album a 'bore': 'It's no surprise that as they run out of things to say – all this adds to our insight into interpersonals, is a few turns of phrase – they figure out artier ways of saying them.' But Christgau praised 'Long Distance Love': 'I'd recommend to Wilson Pickett though.' So did Peter Erskine of *New Musical Express* (*NME*), who opened his review with 'The last time I wept this much, was on my sixth birthday,' before spending a generous five paragraphs on a surprisingly touching accolade. The rest of the album was just as positively received:

There are those who, on hearing this album, will undoubtedly gripe at Lowell George's increasingly-low profile, arguing that group democracy will only lead Little Feat into absorption and disappearance into the mainstream. *The Last Record Album* is however a momentous album for Little Feat, because *group democracy* has lent new fervor to all elements of the band, whilst relieving some of the pressure on George, allowing him to distill the volume of his output into its quintessentially-finest form.

Erskine concluded that the album 'is doubly momentous for Little Feat because it will in fact be their first big hit, because they've managed to combine the stilted tangential feeling of their hitherto best – *Sailin' Shoes* – with the more immediate (but again stilted) and easily-assimilated black-funk feel of *Feats*. Boys, ah jus' loves ya t' death.'

In *Time Out*, Myles Palmer concluded his generally complimentary review with 'I look forward early to their next five albums,' capturing the mood of the album perfectly: '*Feats Don't Fail Me Now* was body music. This is late-night head music: much looser, more laid-back, six men jamming with supreme stoned rapport.' Even if that wasn't actually how the sessions went down, George's production was in line with the hazy, summery vibe of Los Angeles in 1975, made all the more prominent with Neon Park's typically-abstract cover – a surreal Hollywood Boulevard landscape, with a smirking antlered jackrabbit perched in front of cacti, Frederick's of Hollywood and the Pussycat Theatre, while Mount Lee has been replaced with a giant Jell-o mold with a dollop of whipped cream on top. Payne later said, 'Paul says Hollywood is nothing but a fruit dessert with Cool Whip.'

So, after all the hullabaloo around their supposed palace revolution, how did the album's masterminds feel about it? Payne wasn't thrilled with it at the time, telling *Streetlife*: 'I don't want to bad-rap the album. I like it. But it wasn't quite what I hoped for.' With the benefit of 25 years of hindsight, Barrère told Scoppa: 'The record always seemed so compressed, clean, very pristine, stifled.'

'Romance Dance' (Paul Barrère, Kenny Gradney, Bill Payne)
US B-side (WBS-8219), 21 January 1976; UK B-side (K16689), February 1976

Songs about boredom are rarely good, and songs about boredom that leads to sex aren't much better, but this album opener proves an exception. This song is not a classic by any stretch of the imagination, but from its syncopated opening rhythm – capturing a few magical moments where the band feels around for the groove before settling in – this still embodies the spirit of the first four albums.

The song wasn't exactly a live favorite, though it was a regular in the tour setlist, with a post-first-chorus instrumental passage that was cut from the studio recording (listen for the edit at around 1:19) and Payne usually meeting a 'whore from Juarez' instead of just a girl. Future performances were less frequent, with a virtual two-year absence before it returned for two surprise plays in April and May 1978. Sadly, this meant this underrated gem wasn't captured for the live album *Waiting for Columbus*, but a handful of performances are available to listen to on archive.org.

'All That You Dream' (Paul Barrère, Bill Payne)
US A-side (WBS-8219), 26 May 1976

If there was any justice in this world, this song – with its sunny production and infectious chorus – would've been the hit single of summer 1976. Okay, perhaps 'I've been down but not like this before' might've been an odd hook for a hit single, but the song is just another example of the band aiming for the charts and missing through no fault of their own.

Written primarily by Barrère, and first demoed in the *Feats Don't Fail Me Now* sessions (that version eventually released in the *Hotcakes* box set), Payne finessed the song during *The Last Record Album* sessions, though it nearly didn't make it. Barrère recalled in the *Hotcakes* liner notes: 'For the longest time I couldn't convince Lowell that this was a good tune, and thankfully after we recorded this demo, George (Massenburg) told me he would whistle the hook around the studio when he and Lowell were working. Finally, Lowell asked, 'What the fuck is that?!', and so (Massenburg) played him this raw demo … we finally got around to recording on the next record.'

While it's unfair to compare the raw demo with the polished studio recording, the most obvious decision was having George sing lead instead of

Barrère. Not that Barrère is a bad singer, but George's voice – at its peak in 1975 – inarguably improved the recording, taking it from good to great. The single (b/w 'One Love Stand') was an entirely new recording – albeit mixed in mono – and remained unavailable on CD until the *Hotcakes* box set.

'Long Distance Love' (Lowell George)
US A-side (WBS-8219), 21 January 1976; UK A-side (K16689), February 1976

It's been argued that due to George's continuous substance abuse and overall lethargy, he was unable to write a song on the level of his previous heavyweights, but this track is irrefutable proof against that argument. Clocking in just under three minutes, it's an exercise in simplicity, as the focus is on George's voice (with backing vocalists Valerie Carter and Fran Tate). Only Payne and George offer any major embellishment – the former with electric piano, the latter with a brief slide guitar solo.

George originally submitted the song for the *Feats* album, with a version recorded but not released. A few solo recordings with an additional verse, float around in collectors' circles, but whether this was the original *Feats* recording or a demo, is unknown. 'Long Distance Love' b/w 'Romance Dance' was issued in January 1976 as the album's first US single, though, predictably, it failed to chart. The following month, the same pairing was issued in the UK, with a clip of the band recording the song during tour rehearsals at the Alley in North Hollywood airing on *The Old Grey Whistle Test*, and while many Feats fans recall tuning in to watch it, it wasn't enough to give the band a much-needed hit single.

'Day Or Night' (Bill Payne, Fran Tate)
No stronger example of Little Feat's move into jazz-rock territory exists than this – their longest song to date (Only the two medleys 'Cold Cold Cold/Tripe Face Boogie' and 'Forty-Four Blues/How Many More Years' are longer), and the precursor to the even-more-reviled 'Day At The Dog Races.' Written by Payne and his girlfriend Fran Tate, the song really wasn't too much of a departure – lyrically it recalled 'Walkin' All Night,' with Payne's narrator in search of a good time ('There ain't no Jane, no Jill, no Sally/To see you through'; 'Maybe you'll find your way today/But while you're at it you'll have some fun'), while its arrangement owed a lot to the progressive leanings of 'The Fan.'

To his credit, George liked the song, though if he played guitar on the recording, it's difficult to tell. He was likely situated in the control room while the band raged on, leaving much of the embellishments to Payne, who offers up a few interesting synthesizer sounds. The real star of the show is Hayward, who maintained to Fong-Torres that 'I kinda liked both Lowell's and Billy's directions, so I acted as the pressure-relief in the band.' His drumming here is exemplary, turning in a superhuman performance that is tight but loose; flashy yet restrained. The final 94 seconds are a testament to his talent and tenacity, with a lengthy solo feature that fades away, only to fade back in for the real ending.

Like most of Payne's latter-day compositions, 'Day Or Night' evolved from rehearsals and soundchecks, with an embryonic (but mostly fully-realized) version performed in Atlanta on 23 May 1975. After the album was released, the song became an established live staple, with over 400 known performances – often in conjunction with 'Time Loves A Hero,' but occasionally 'Juliette' or 'Lafayette Railroad.' A good example of this is on *Waiting for Columbus* – a performance that also benefits from the additions of George on slide guitar and Tower of Power's Lenny Pickett on saxophone.

'One Love Stand' (Paul Barrère, Kenny Gradney, Bill Payne)
US B-side (WBS-8219), 26 May 1976

Another funky boogie shuffle that benefits from George's engagement, with a stellar, emotional lead vocal and some scorching slide guitar. Payne and Barrère's lyrics are unusually honest – perhaps the result of both entering serious relationships (the former with Fran Tate, the latter with Debbie Donovan). The accomplished composition slipped out as the US B-side to 'All That You Dream,' though it earned more prominence in the live setlist – often as part of a medley with 'Rock And Roll Doctor.' Except for two airings in 2001, 'One Love Stand' hasn't been played live since 9 August 1977: happily, this was recorded and later released as a bonus track on the expanded *Waiting for Columbus* reissue.

'Down Below The Borderline' (Lowell George)
Not one of George's better songs, this nevertheless has a metallic edge that cuts through the album's gloss: making it a worthy inclusion. Unfortunately, the final arrangement was tweaked to be more conventional. George's demo (on the *Hotcakes* box set) features a syncopated Donca Matic rhythm box pattern that provides some much-needed shifts, twists and turns that were smoothed over in the studio version. But there are some redeeming qualities: George's octave vocal is a nice touch, and his singing overall elevates the song from middling to good.

While the album's other songs became concert staples, 'Down Below The Borderline' failed to catch fire in the live setting, surviving for only three known setlists in October and November 1975, though it was brought out of mothballs once in April 1978.

'Somebody's Leavin'' (Bill Payne)
A song of longing, loss and regret, with Payne the detached narrator ('What was it like when you saw your whole life go under?/Why can't two people leave well enough alone?') – though he's clearly the spurned party ('Did you hear me when I told you I loved you?') – this is a minor masterpiece that the album's

higher-profile songs unfairly left in the dust. The band delivers a sublime performance – Payne's piano work is exquisite, especially his solo (boosted by synthesizer and ethereal backing vocals), and Gradney's bass is beautiful and understated. Barrère's rhythm guitar is barely audible, while George joins in on bottleneck towards the end. Only Clayton seems to be absent.

The song's only known live performance came nearly two years before its release, on 3 November 1973 when Little Feat performed a set for Pacifica Radio's KPFT 90.1 FM at Sugar Hill Studios in Houston, Texas. Coincidentally, they also played 'China White,' making for a unique experience, which Payne explained in his show intro: 'We figured that it would be real good to just act as if we were doing a session, and we're gonna do some new and unusual material for you all.' (Incidentally, this was Fred White's second performance on the drum stool after Hayward's dismissal.)

'Mercenary Territory' (Lowell George, Elizabeth George, Richie Hayward)

This is a sublime counterpart to 'Long Distance Love,' except here, the distance is emotional, not physical. George's widow Liz gave herself a belated credit on the *Hotcakes* box set, maintaining that the lyrics were drawn from letters she'd sent to George in times of romantic upheaval: 'I was really bugged at him and wrote him a very strong letter. It inspired the song.'

Indeed, George takes Liz's charges – 'Is it the lies? Is it the style?' – and explains himself without remorse: 'I've been out here so long, dreamin' up songs/Fool that I am, I'd do it all over again.' Though propulsive, 'Mercenary Territory' was perhaps a bit too gentle, as the track fails to come to life. Happily, George believed in the song and worked up a live arrangement just in time for the *Waiting for Columbus* recordings, with an absolutely transcendent performance included on that album.

Related Tracks
'Rockin' Shoes I & II' (Lowell George)

This demo was recorded simultaneously to 'Down Below The Borderline,' with both released in the *Hotcakes* box set. It's a shame Little Feat never recorded this song proper, as it's certainly no worse than anything else submitted for the *Last Record Album* sessions. Barrère certainly liked the song: 'I remember that after Lowell passed away, I called Liz and asked if there were any songs that we had not recorded layin' around, and she gave me a tape of this. So I got together with Martin Kibbee and finished off this song for my second solo project (*Real Lies*).'

Time Loves a Hero (1977)

Personnel:
Paul Barrère: guitar, vocals; co-lead vocal on 'Time Loves A Hero'; lead vocal on 'Old Folks Boogie,' 'Keepin' Up With The Joneses' and 'Missin' You'
Sam Clayton: congas, percussion, vocals
Lowell George: vocals, guitar
Kenny Gradney: bass
Richie Hayward: drums, percussion, vocals
Bill Payne: keyboards, synthesizer, marimba, vocals; co-lead vocal on 'Time Loves A Hero'; lead vocal on 'Red Streamliner'
Additional personnel:
Michael McDonald: backing vocals on 'Red Streamliner'
Patrick Simmons: guitar on 'New Delhi Freight Train'; backing vocals on 'Red Streamliner'
Fred Tackett: mandocello and guitar on 'Time Loves A Hero'
Tower of Power horn section – Greg Adams: trumpet; Emilio Castillo: tenor saxophone; Mic Gillette: trombone, trumpet; Stephen 'Doc' Kupka: baritone saxophone; Lenny Pickett: alto and tenor saxophones: 'Hi Roller,' 'Old Folks Boogie' and 'Keepin' Up With The Joneses'
Recorded at Sunset Sound and Western Recorders, Los Angeles; Warner Bros. Studios, North Hollywood; The Record Plant, Sausalito, Late 1976–early 1977
Producer: Ted Templeman
Release date: US: 15 April 1977
Peak position: US: 34, UK: 8
Running time: 35:27

With each successive album, Little Feat raised their profile considerably. Unfortunately, the flip side of that coin was that the pressure to deliver the goods was intensified. Lenny Waronker and Mo Ostin from Warner Bros. weren't happy that they'd sunk so much money into *The Last Record Album* and gotten only eight songs, a short running time and a rather lifeless production. But sales were still healthy, so Warners couldn't have been *too* unhappy. But Payne and Barrère had their own concerns after a lackluster October-1976 session when the band re-recorded the already-released 'All That You Dream', 'Front Page News' (the perpetual 'Maybe next time'), a remake of 'Roll Um Easy' and a handful of demos for Valerie Carter's *Just a Stone's Throw Away* album (likely the Payne/George/Carter co-write 'Back To Blue Some More,' and possibly 'Heartache,' 'Face Of Appalachia' and 'Cowboy Angel': all of which George co-wrote with others). Uncertain whether George was up to producing the new record on his own, Payne and Barrère informed Waronker and Ostin of their concerns, thus giving Warner Bros. the ammunition they needed to bring in an outside producer.

By 1976, producer Ted Templeman had a higher profile after working with The Doobie Brothers, Van Morrison, Montrose, and more recently Carly

49

Simon (Soon he would become the producer of choice for Van Halen), but he jumped at the chance to work with Little Feat again. He told Bud Scoppa in the *Hotcakes and Outtakes* liner notes: 'It wasn't a matter of green-lighting it, I was just, 'What, are you kidding?'. I was more for it than Lenny, 'cause he was always a Lowell guy. Lenny just didn't get Billy as much. I just said, 'Fuck yeah.' And I knew Lowell would come around and add to it.'

George eventually did come around, but only just. It seemed there was more to blame than just disillusionment with success: George wasn't taking care of himself. Not only had he pulled a Hayward and crashed his motorcycle – laying him up in hospital for a bit (Tellingly there were no medical bills plastered over the new album's rear sleeve) – but his drug abuse had increased so much that he'd gained considerable weight and contracted hepatitis C.

It's no surprise then that Barrère and Payne had to step up and guide the band, or else there wouldn't be a band to guide. 'We're not breaking up. There's no way,' Barrère firmly assured *Circus* magazine in June 1977, before pulling the curtain back further and getting to the real reason: 'It would cost us too much ... due to our contract.' Besides, George had been asking for help since *Feats Don't Fail Me Now*, and Barrère and Payne had finally taken him up on it on *The Last Record Album*, so it made sense that if George was going to be preoccupied with outside endeavors – and not with getting healthy – then the dynamic would have to shift in order to keep the band alive.

But George was still precious about his role as a producer, and when Payne told George that he felt he was owed more production input, he was rejected, which only pushed the pair further apart. With Barrère stepping up with his own songwriting (writing or co-writing six of the nine tracks) and George stepping back (one solo and one co-write with Barrère), the natural conclusion seemed to be that Barrère and Payne had staged a coup and usurped George – he even insinuated such in his final interview with Bill Flanagan, which did a lot of damage to Barrère and Payne. Barrère simply said, 'He wanted us to do more, but he wanted the control ... Lowell was still kind of holding on to it all, even though he had told us that 'You guys need to step up and participate more.' And then when we did, it was a shock to him.'

At least *Time Loves a Hero* had more of a pulse than *The Last Record Album*, even though the sound and mood was closer to that album than it was to early Feats. It helped that the sessions went relatively smoothly, despite the protracted length (October 1976 to February 1977). Barrère attributed this to a more structured schedule, with sessions running from noon to six in the evening. However, George was frequently absent, for a valid reason beyond his ailing health: Warner Bros. wanted his long-promised solo record, so he focused his attention more on that. Instead of grumbling about it, the band worked on Barrère and Payne's songs, determined to get an album out one way or another.

With Templeman, Payne and Barrère again had a sympathetic ear – especially Payne, who brought the embryo of 'Day At The Dog Races' to rehearsal. Templeman immediately connected with the groove, and again with the band.

He told Fong-Torres: 'They were kickin' ass. Billy had hit his creative stride, and Paul too. I was just sittin' back and letting Billy roll.' George had his reservations about the song at the time but recognized he was outnumbered and didn't oppose its inclusion. Instead, he saved it for the press, denigrating Payne's jazz-fusion leanings whenever possible. Barrère regretted the communication breakdown, admitting to Fong-Torres, 'Looking back on it, probably we should have stayed in better contact – discussed whatever it was that was causing problems and so forth.'

Time Loves a Hero was finally released in April 1977: 18 months after their last album. Whether critics and fans were starved for new Feats, or it just happened to resonate strongly, the album reached number 34 in the US: two better than its predecessor. Across the pond, the album soared into the top 10, no doubt assisted by the band's extensive live campaign of the previous year. The album's critical reception matched its commercial success. *Rolling Stone*'s Peter Herbst liked it better than its predecessor, praising Payne and Barrère's aspirations: 'The new material not only takes advantage of a strong, flexible rhythm section but also provides better melodies than did the previous two albums.' *Rock Around the World*'s Don Snowden went one further, calling it 'excellent' and specifically praising 'Day At The Dog Races' and 'Old Folks Boogie.' The UK press were equally effusive – *Melody Maker* called it 'The band's best album to date'; *Sounds* insisted it was 'cut-to-cut crammed with classics.' Tellingly, the *NME* blasted George's absence – '(He) has all but forsaken his writing chores, and it hardly matters' – enthusing that the album 'certainly makes a monkey out of most other records released this year.'

If George was upset, he didn't let it show. In 2002, Van Dyke Parks told Mark Brend that George 'reacted like a kid who got high praise on a test after no preparation'. It seemed to be enough to kick him back into gear – just after the album was released, he told the band that he was interested in them recording a definitive live album. The others – especially Payne and Barrère – breathed a sigh of relief: their leader had returned to take the wheel.

'Hi Roller' (Paul Barrère)
This long-delayed 'maybe next time' finally got its release. Fans were treated to the lyrics on the *Last Record Album* rear sleeve, though it wasn't until 2000 that a previously unreleased take (known as 'Ace In The Hole') from the *Dixie Chicken* sessions slipped out on the *Hotcakes* box set – as did the 1975 version: for those curious how *The Last Record Album* would have sounded with its inclusion. (Barrère also recorded the song for his 1983 debut solo album *On My Own Two Feet*, with an arrangement closer to the 1975 version.)

Inspired by a hitchhiking trip to Lake Tahoe that Barrère took with his friend Low-Ball Jack ('To say the least, we certainly didn't win anything at the tables because we wound up sleeping outside in a campground. But when you're 18 years old, who cared!!!'), the song is a defiant album opener, with a thundering drum fill leading into a funky rocker with heavy wah-wah guitar and throaty brass. While the horns occasionally steer the track into cheap B-movie cop-flick territory, it's one of the album's more energetic tracks. But it was an infrequent setlist addition, with only 13 performances in George's lifetime and a further 76 between 1998 and 2019.

'Time Loves A Hero' (Paul Barrère, Kenny Gradney, Bill Payne)
US A-side (WBS-8420), 3 August 1977

The title track is another sleek and funky slice of whimsy, with Barrère and Payne taking the lead on lyrics and vocals, telling the story of an uncle who ups sticks to Puerto Rico, leaving behind a heartbroken wife. He's labeled a coward, but the narrator forgives it with a shrug, unable to find any fault with 'bumming around the beaches of Puerto Rico.' The narrator admits, 'As a coward, I admire his courageous ways,' and concludes with 'Better San Juan than that blue-collar hell.'

Due to George's absence, Fred Tackett played guitar and mandocello, though live performances benefited greatly from George's bottleneck. The track was also the album's sole single (b/w 'Sailin' Shoes'), but the public showed no interest whatsoever. The song was an immediate live favorite, though – with 530 documented performances – and was often followed by 'Day Or Night.'

'Rocket In My Pocket' (Lowell George)
George's sole contribution to the album is this lascivious, lustful mid-tempo rocker – taken perhaps a tad too slowly, though it bursts to life in the choruses. The production does the song a disservice, as it's far too clean and precise, though George's heavily-treated slide guitar work brings some grit, at times dueling with Payne's synthesizer embellishments. But as beloved as the song is, it's more or less George-by-numbers – consisting of two verses, a half verse and one chorus repeated twice. He doesn't really say much here, though he does get in one good final couplet: 'She got one foot on the platform/And the other is on the train.'

Any shortcomings the recording may have had were rectified onstage, with a particularly scorching version captured at the Rainbow Theatre and released on *Waiting for Columbus.* The Tower of Power horns certainly helped take the song to another stratosphere, but even unadorned – as on Feats' 1977 *Midnight Special* appearance – it benefited simply from a fully-engaged George, with the band firing on all cylinders behind him. The song was played nearly every night on the 1977 and 1978 tours, and was one of a handful of Feats songs that George integrated into his solo tour.

'Day At The Dog Races' (Paul Barrère, Sam Clayton, Kenny Gradney, Richie Hayward, Bill Payne)
George hadn't taken a liking to the jazz-fusion elements that Payne brought to the Feats sound, and, reportedly, upon hearing a playback of the instrumental

'Day At The Dog Races,' exasperatedly shouted to producer Ted Templeman, 'What is this? Fuckin' Weather Report?'. Payne recalled to Ben Fong-Torres: 'Lowell hated it for some reason. He thought it was just too fusion-like, so he'd go offstage while we'd play it.' To his credit, Payne wasn't bothered by George's absence: 'I just figured, *when in doubt, lay out*. If you don't like it, don't play it.'

George didn't always lay out, however. The song had its origins in Payne's 'Tripe Face Boogie' keyboard solo as far back as November 1973, with a trio of (known) performances popping up before the song became a concert staple. But it still needed some polishing, and Payne – unwilling to let a good groove go – brought the song to rehearsal (which George typically avoided) for the others to work on. He told Fong-Torres: 'Sam and Kenny and Richie were having their connection on the rhythm side, and Billy and I were having a connection melodically that was just phenomenal. We had a ball doing that kind of stuff. I don't know if that's what flipped Lowell out, but he was not totally sold on that kind of thing … He thought we were just kind of copying Weather Report in a certain fashion. I didn't see it that way at all. I just saw it as another step musically, to have fun.'

While Payne later admitted to 'taking my cues from Joe Zawinul of Weather Report,' he insists he wasn't trying to mold Little Feat into a jazz-fusion outfit, saying in the *Hotcakes* liner notes: 'Look, every step of the way we've bastardized everything we've done. Very little of what Little Feat does is original, but what makes it Little Feat, is this voice we have behind it. We've never been afraid to take certain elements and mix them up.'

George just couldn't stand it, plain and simple; telling Bill Flanagan on 17 June 1979 in his final interview: 'If you shoot at something and you know it ain't gonna make it, why bother? … Occasionally it made it though. I would say that later on, one out of six was real hot and came across. But the other five, you had to sit through.'

For all the disdain the track gets, it's really not that bad. There are enough interesting elements, whether it's Payne's various keyboard parts (Oberheim synthesizer, electric and acoustic piano), Barrère offering up some crunchy, almost metallic guitar riffs, or the rhythm section settling into the groove while allowing enough room to have their own fun. Hayward especially shines on drums – effortlessly throwing in rolls or cymbal crashes while maintaining the complicated rhythm. Perhaps the problem is that fans thought the band were taking themselves too seriously, and even George seems to have bought into (or and even fueled) this angle. But from the song title to the over-the-top Oberheim introduction, it's obvious the band is just having a good time, and anyone who had ever seen Little Feat live, knew they hardly took themselves seriously. Further to this, considering the tumultuous recording sessions and having to deal with an absent leader who had no problem criticizing his bandmates' songs yet could only be bothered to write one complete song when requested, the others could hardly be blamed for wanting to let off steam and get into a good groove.

With the benefit of hindsight, Ted Templeman revised his story to Fong-Torres in 2013, insisting that reports of George's dislike of the song were over-exaggerated: 'He was so easygoing. He didn't say, 'What are you trying to do? Be Weather Report?' I liked it ... nobody ever raised their voice.'

'Old Folks Boogie' (Paul Barrère, Gabriel Barrère)

Once again reduced to a quintet, the band turned in a stellar version of Barrère's cynically-twisted take on the aging process. Inspired by a joke his father Gabriel (a one-time New York vaudeville theater usher) used to tell at home ('You know that you're over the hill/When your mind makes a promise that your body can't fill'), this is perhaps one of Barrère's finest and sharpest songs – a nice balance between Payne's more lofty ambitions and George's aloofness.

The arrangement is especially inspired, starting off with a syncopated stop/start rhythm reminiscent of 'Rock And Roll Doctor,' before ending with the seductive shuffling of 'Tripe Face Boogie' and 'Dixie Chicken' (except the only shuffling going on here is into slippers). The track plods, but not to its detriment, as it gives the listener ample time and space to appreciate the words: each line like the punchline to a joke that's been told a thousand times.

Later a live favorite, 'Old Folks Boogie' featured on *Waiting for Columbus*, with the Tower of Power horns masterfully executing the 'tumbling down the stairs' finale. Some live performances before and since – with or without a horn section – weren't so graceful, which I suppose only adds to the charm!

'Red Streamliner' (Bill Payne, Fran Tate)

While visiting his parents in Moody, Texas, Payne was struggling to fall asleep when he heard a train whistle off in the distance. He wrote in the *Hoy-Hoy!* liner notes: 'Everything else was so quiet that the whistle created all these images of the railroad industry, which was then starting to fall apart. A fast romantic link with American history.'

Though the title imagery suggests a *Dixie Chicken* outtake, the actual performance is Little Feat at its slickest, with Gradney's slinky bass line, and silky-smooth backing vocals from The Doobie Brothers' Patrick Simmons and Michael McDonald. Only Payne's synthesizers – especially the stifling solo – now border on the dated, but it's still superb.

Unfortunately, on this track, George was once again absent – which is a shame, as railway lyrics and bottleneck guitar are synonymous with each other. At least the live outtake features George's particularly scorching slide contribution – recorded during the *Waiting for Columbus* concerts but held back until *Hoy-Hoy!* (later on, the expanded *Columbus* reissue).

'New Delhi Freight Train' (Terry Allen)

As 'Red Streamliner' fades out, this rattler pulls into the station. George brought it to the sessions out of either desperation for one more song, appreciation for it, or perhaps a bit of both. George is engaged, turning in a stellar vocal, even punctuating the otherwise plodding arrangement with some stinging slide guitar. However, the track drags, and the band have been so drastically sanitized that they sound like session musicians. The track might've been more appropriate on George's solo album *Thanks, I'll Eat It Here*.

Songwriter Terry Allen – a friend of George's – released his own version two years later on his stellar double album *Lubbock (on everything)*, and opened its follow-up *Smokin' the Dummy* with 'The Heart Of California (For Lowell George).'

'Keepin' Up With the Joneses' (Paul Barrère, Lowell George)

Side two starts strong but drags in the middle, with two of the most laborious arrangements sequenced back-to-back. While 'New Delhi Freight Train' worked well as a mood piece (and had the benefit of George's presence), this track is a struggle to get through, even though certain elements are superb: Hayward's inventive drumming, the Tower of Power horn section (Especially Lenny Pickett's brief but impassioned solo) and Barrère's vocal. Surprisingly, George makes no audible contribution.

The song was performed once on tour in 1977 and was a regular on the autumn-1978 tour. It was even pulled out of mothballs after the band reformed, becoming a semi-staple of the set between 1992 and 2019.

'Missin' You' (Paul Barrère)

The album closes with this simple acoustic lament: written, sung and performed entirely by Barrère. Jeff 'Skunk' Baxter was credited with dobro, which Barrère corrected in 2002: 'The skunk was not on that track.'

Whether written about a lover or a friend, Barrère abides by the idea that simple is better, and keeps the message universal. Only in the verse ('Nashville at sunrise/Rain's poundin' on my window') does it become a little more personal.

Notably, this was the last-released Little Feat studio album track in Lowell George's lifetime, which only further cements the song's poignancy. The song wouldn't be performed live until 2002, with only five performances between May and October. Its most recent performance was on 25 January 2020, three months after Barrère's death, played in dedication to him at Little Feat's Ramble On the Island in Jamaica.

Waiting for Columbus (1978)

Personnel:
Paul Barrère: guitar, vocals
Sam Clayton: congas, percussion, vocals
Lowell George: vocals, guitar, maraca, cowbell
Kenny Gradney: bass
Richie Hayward: drums, vocals
Bill Payne: acoustic and electric piano, organ, synthesizer, vocals
Additional personnel:
Mic Gillette: 1st trumpet, trombone
Greg Adams: 2nd trumpet, horn arrangements
Lenny Pickett: 1st tenor saxophone, alto saxophone (solos)
Emilio Castillo: 2nd tenor saxophone
Stephen 'Doc' Kupka: baritone saxophone
Don 'Cerphe' Colwell: emcee
Recording information is noted below after individual songs.
Producer: Lowell George
Release date: US: 10 February 1978
Peak position: US: 18, UK: 43
Running time: 81:38

While the first iteration of Little Feat did have their onstage moments, it wasn't until Barrère, Gradney and Clayton joined that the band were able to achieve truly great heights. Before long, they were a well-oiled machine in concert, allowing them room to stretch a song out, flow effortlessly from one song into another, or even try out new ideas in front of a rapt audience. Yet there was very little of the posing and posturing of other bands – solos were rarely excessive or indulgent, and when they *were*, they lasted a minute or two at most. The band served as just that: a band. George went to great lengths to ensure that Little Feat was a democracy and contributions were welcome from everyone.

Except when they weren't. George had ceded control to Payne and Barrère on *Time Loves a Hero*, which ended up becoming one of their most successful albums. Whether George recognized he was in danger of losing his band for good, or just didn't want to spend more time in the studio than he had to, he suggested they record some of their summer concerts and release a live album. Surprised at this sudden burst of interest, the others happily agreed, Payne and Barrère especially thrilled that their erstwhile leader had snapped out of his stupor.

They played a trio of warm-up dates in Newcastle and Manchester, before the mobile recording machines started rolling on 1 August 1977 at London's Rainbow Theatre. (Manchester was actually recorded, but nothing from that show (nor the first night at the Rainbow) made it to the album.) The second night was a momentous occasion. Former Rolling Stones guitarist Mick

Taylor sat in on slide guitar on 'A Apolitical Blues,' and the band delivered an absolutely scorching set. After the show, drinks were poured, lines were cut, and the party continued well into the early hours.

George, Hayward and Barrère showed up at that night's soundcheck pathetically hungover. With the mood already sour and the show about to start, tensions were raised when George and Hayward got into a fight in the hallway. Barrère was still drunk, and – according to those who were there – could barely play. The others were furious, and the date has gone down in Feats lore as 'Black Wednesday.' To his credit, Barrère admitted his faults and vowed to never repeat the same mistake.

Things went a little smoother once the band returned stateside, with another trio of shows at the Washington, D.C. Lisner Auditorium. Nine of the album's tracks were pulled from these dates, while the other eight came from the Rainbow. Black Wednesday was ignored for the most part, with only (most of) 'Dixie Chicken,' the piano solo from 'Tripe Face Boogie,' and 'A Apolitical Blues' deemed worthy enough for release.

Between 19 August and 10 September, George bounced between Sunset Sound and Westlake Audio, with George Massenburg and Warren Dewey (who'd recorded the shows in London and D.C. respectively) helping select the best performances: in most cases, they selected themselves. George took the unorthodox step to re-record all of his vocals, then decide on the original, the re-record, or a combination of both (In some instances, you can hear his live vocal bleeding in underneath the re-recorded vocal). In some cases, only the occasional vocal or guitar overdub was necessary. Payne wasn't needed for any keyboard overdubs, and Hayward was only requested for a minor drum fix.

The album was mixed at Westlake between 12 September and 16 October 1977, with 22 songs chosen. In the end, five songs – 'One Love Stand,' 'Rock And Roll Doctor,' 'Skin It Back' (from the Rainbow), 'On Your Way Down' and 'Walkin' All Night' – were cast aside. 'Skin It Back' (from Lisner), 'Red Streamliner' and 'Teenage Nervous Breakdown' were dusted off and mixed in 1980 for *Hoy-Hoy!*. 'Cold, Cold, Cold' and 'Day At The Dog Races' were the only two songs not mixed or considered for the original release but finally appeared as bonus tracks (alongside the aforementioned outtakes) on the album's 2002 CD reissue.

Adorned in a typically out-there Neon Park sleeve (A seductress with a giant tomato for a head, lounges in a hammock), *Waiting for Columbus* earned respectable sales yet middling reviews:

Little Feat's contrariness emerges as energy, and, though this double live set contains fifteen familiar cuts and two quick novelty numbers, it's anything but a garage sale – the songs really smoke. (*Rolling Stone*)

Feats do fail us now and again. (*Melody Maker*)

NME in the UK called the album 'a tombstone' – peaking at number 43: not resonating there as much as *Time Loves a Hero* had. Sales were more promising in the US, earning Little Feat their first (and only) top 20 album.

But time has been kind to the album, and by the early 2000s – with Little Feat's star again on the rise – it was given the deluxe treatment: frustratingly, the only Little Feat album to date to receive such an honor. In Bud Scoppa's superb liner notes – which balance that fine line between unduly unctuous and inordinately informative – comparisons are drawn with such classics as The Who's *Live at Leeds*, The Band's *Rock of Ages* and The Allman Brothers Band's *At Fillmore East*, and it's not too far-fetched. All demonstrate their respective musicians at their (arguable) peak, and the performances improve on their studio counterparts: either through different arrangements or just because the band happened to have a good night.

More often than not, Little Feat had good nights, but they were becoming increasingly rare by 1977. Incidentally, the response to *Waiting for Columbus* was so positive, the band had to go on tour to promote it, and their spring and summer shows of 1978 were surprisingly inspired. While there are more electrifying (and complete) performances (notably the two 1973 and 1974 radio performances for WLIR), *Waiting for Columbus* captures the most infamous Little Feat just past their prime, yet still absolutely stunning overall. It was so career-defining, they didn't release another live album for over a decade.

'Join The Band' (trad; arr. Little Feat)
Recorded at Lisner Auditorium, Washington, D.C., 10 August 1977

One of Little Feat's pre-show rituals was to sing the traditional *a cappella* chain-gang chant 'Join The Band' as they walked from the dressing room to the stage. Warren Dewey – who recorded the Lisner shows – took note and set up microphones in the hallways on their final night in D.C., giving the listener the experience of following the band to the stage.

'Fat Man In The Bathtub' (Lowell George)
Recorded at Lisner Auditorium, Washington, D.C., 8 August 1977

WHFS DJ Don 'Cerphe' Colwell greets the audience and hypes them up, before George starts the cowbell intro of the *Dixie Chicken* favorite – serving as a particularly effective album opener, even if it never actually opened any of the recorded concerts (That task went to 'Skin It Back' or 'Walkin' All Night').

'All That You Dream' (Paul Barrère, Bill Payne)
Recorded at Lisner Auditorium, Washington, D.C., 8 August 1977

The sunny-if-laid-back studio arrangement is transformed with a faster tempo, featuring George's stinging slide contribution. Hayward's drums are also especially mighty.

'Oh Atlanta' (Bill Payne)
Recorded at Lisner Auditorium, Washington, D.C., 8 August 1977. Payne: vocal. US A-side (WBS-8566), April 1978

The hit single that never was benefits from a more-robust arrangement and Payne's insistence on using a baby-grand piano instead of the more practical and portable electric piano: 'much against the desires of the crew, I might add!', he noted to Scoppa in the reissue liner notes. Released as the album's only single – b/w 'Willin'' – 'Oh Atlanta' predictably failed to chart.

'Old Folks Boogie' (Paul Barrère, Gabriel Barrère)
Recorded at the Rainbow Theatre, London, 4 August 1977. Barrère: vocal

Barrère gets his turn to sing, and the band is tight. But it's the last 90 seconds that prove the musical chemistry and intuition were still there.

'Time Loves A Hero' (Paul Barrère, Kenny Gradney, Bill Payne)
Recorded at the Rainbow Theatre, London, 4 August 1977. Barrère and Payne: vocals

Side two opens with this rather straightforward performance. If it weren't for the segue into the superb 'Day Or Night', this could've been dropped from the running order, without being missed.

'Day Or Night' (Bill Payne, Fran Tate)
Recorded at the Rainbow Theatre, London, 4 August 1977. Barrère and Payne: vocals

This performance benefits not only from George's presence, but also that of Tower of Power's Lenny Pickett, whose impressive saxophone solo, pushes the band – especially Hayward – to greater heights.

'Mercenary Territory' (Lowell George, Richie Hayward)
Recorded at the Rainbow Theatre, London, 2 August 1977

If ever there was proof of Little Feat's prowess as a live band, this is it. The limp and plodding *Last Record Album* closer is transformed into an absolute powerhouse, aided by the Tower of Power horns – especially Lenny Pickett, whose improvised sax solo matches George's impassioned vocal and slide solo. Barrère called it 'One of the most classic live moments captured *ever*,' and it's hard to disagree with him. Except – according to Payne in the *Hotcakes* liner notes – this wasn't actually the concert performance but was extracted from the soundcheck, and sweetened up later.

Or *was* it? Listening to the available band-sanctioned soundboard recordings of this concert uploaded on *archive.org*, I can't tell much of a difference in the instrumental performance, though George obviously re-recorded his vocal, and some guitar retouching was necessary. (Pickett's solo sounds exactly the same, though it was mixed higher for the album.)

'Spanish Moon' (Lowell George)
Recorded at Lisner Auditorium, Washington, D.C., 8 August 1977

The Tower of Power horns had already guested on the studio version of 'Spanish Moon,' so it was no surprise their appearance here boosted an already electrifying performance. (This concluded side two of the original vinyl release, but for the expanded 2002 CD reissue, sides two and three (side three being 'Dixie Chicken,' 'Tripe Face Boogie' and 'Rocket in My Pocket') were swapped to allow the long fade-out of 'Spanish Moon' to end disc 1.)

'Dixie Chicken' (Lowell George, Martin Kibbee)
Recorded at the Rainbow Theatre, London, 3 and 4 August 1977. Lenny Pickett: clarinet

A highlight among highlights, this starts off modestly enough, with an extemporizing Payne tickling the ivories as a precursor to an otherwise-straightforward performance. But then the Tower of Power horn section turn into a New Orleans brass band, tootlin' and wailin' away, before settling back into the languid pace. After nearly nine minutes of pure musical joy, the tempo picks up …

'Tripe Face Boogie' (Richie Hayward, Bill Payne)
Recorded at the Rainbow Theatre, London, 2 and 3 August 1977

…and this *Sailin' Shoes* favorite kicks into gear – again, mostly straightforward until Payne lays on a thick Oberheim synthesizer solo and leads the band into jazz fusion territory, with elements of 'Day At The Dog Races' interwoven.

'Rocket In My Pocket' (Lowell George)
Recorded at the Rainbow Theatre, London, 2 August 1977

George's sole contribution to *Time Loves a Hero* is given a more beefy arrangement, with the Tower of Power horns in full flight.

'Willin'' (Lowell George)
Recorded at Lisner Auditorium, Washington, D.C., 8 August 1977. US B-side (WBS-8566), April 1978

'You folks are crazy!' a delighted George utters as the D.C. audience goes nuts.

But they quickly quieten down for the now-customary encore, which sticks fairly close to the *Sailin' Shoes* arrangement.

'Don't Bogart That Joint' (Elliot Ingber, Larry Wagner)
Recorded at Lisner Auditorium, Washington, D.C., 8 August 1977

The only *new* song on the album, this was first released as 'Don't Bogart Me' on Fraternity of Man's eponymous 1968 debut – that version gaining considerable prominence as part of the influential *Easy Rider* film and soundtrack. Here, the song was woven into 'Willin'' and the band introductions on these dates (though it was performed earlier in the year). But with some clever surgery, the medley became two separate songs on the album

'A Apolitical Blues' (Lowell George)
Recorded at the Rainbow Theatre, London, 3 August 1977. Mick Taylor: slide guitar

Former Rolling Stone Mick Taylor stopped by to duel with George on slide guitar for this *Sailin' Shoes* favorite, though George ran circles around their guest.

'Sailin' Shoes' (Lowell George)
Recorded at Lisner Auditorium, Washington, D.C., 10 August 1977

This lengthy performance dances beautifully between stoned stupor and scorching excitement.

'Feats Don't Fail Me Now' (Paul Barrère, Lowell George, Martin Kibbee)
Recorded at Lisner Auditorium, Washington, D.C., 9 August 1977

This concluded the original album, extended with an instrumental breakdown and raucous call-and-response vocals between George and the vociferous Lisner audience.

Related Tracks
'One Love Stand' (Paul Barrère, Kenny Gradney, Bill Payne)
Recorded at Lisner Auditorium, Washington, D.C., 9 August 1977. Barrère, George, and Payne: vocals

It's a shame this superb performance of the outstanding *Last Record Album* track couldn't have been shoehorned in somewhere on *Waiting for Columbus*, but economy was part of the challenge.

'Rock And Roll Doctor' (Lowell George, Martin Kibbee)
Recorded at Lisner Auditorium, Washington, D.C., 9 August 1977

This performance would've had to be included too, as the above 'One Love Stand' segued effortlessly into it, and that's another four minutes of space to find somewhere.

'Skin It Back' (Barrère)
Recorded at the Rainbow Theatre, London, 2 August 1977. Barrère: vocal

Mixed for the original album but rejected, this features a full ending – as opposed to the Lisner version mixed in 1980 for *Hoy-Hoy!*, which faded out before the segue into 'Fat Man In The Bathtub.'

'On Your Way Down' (Allen Toussaint)
Recorded at Lisner Auditorium, Washington, D.C., 10 August 1977

Little Feat always put a little more emotion and passion into this Allen Toussaint cover, and this performance is no exception.

'Walkin' All Night' (Paul Barrère, Bill Payne)
Recorded at Lisner Auditorium, Washington, D.C., 8 August 1977. Barrère and Payne: vocals

This forgotten relic from simpler times was dusted off as the concert opener on six of the ten dates, yet it eluded release for nearly 25 years. At least it's a fun performance.

'Cold, Cold, Cold' (Lowell George)
Recorded at the Rainbow Theatre, London, 4 August 1977

Another blast from the past, this was in danger of sounding too archaic compared to the newer, slicker Little Feat. But the arrangement was fairly malleable, with the Tower of Power horns adding some much-needed oomph.

'Day At The Dog Races' (Paul Barrère, Sam Clayton, Kenny Gradney, Richie Hayward, Bill Payne)
Recorded at Lisner Auditorium, Washington, D.C., 9 August 1977

Love it or loathe it, this is given a 12-minute workout that is nothing if not impressive.

Thanks, I'll Eat It Here (Lowell George) (1979)

Personnel:
Lowell George: vocals, guitars
Additional personnel:
Bobby Bruce: guitar, violin
Keyboards: Denny Christianson, Luis Damian, Gordon DeWitty, David Foster, Nicky
Hopkins, James Newton Howard, David Paich, Dean Parks, Bruce Paulson, Bill
Payne
Piano: Gordon DeWitty, Maxine Dixon, Arthur Gerst, Jimmy Greenspoon, Peggy
Sandvig
Bass: Dennis Belfield, Chuck Rainey, J.D. Souther, Paul Stallworth
Drums: Michael Baird, Chilli Charles, Jim Gordon, Roberto Gutierrez, Richie
Hayward, Jim Keltner, John Phillips, Jeff Porcaro, Floyd Sneed
Guitar: Turner Stephen Bruton, Luis Damian, Jimmy Greenspoon, Roberto
Gutierrez, Jerry Jumonville, Ron Koss, Dean Parks, Paul Stallworth, Fred Tackett
Horns: Denny Christianson, Darrell Leonard, Steve Madaio, Jim Price
Saxophones: Jerry Jumonville, Joel Peskin, John Phillips
Backing vocals: Roberto Gutierrez, Darrell Leonard, Maxayn Lewis, Bill Payne,
Herb Pedersen, Joel Peskin, Bonnie Raitt, Floyd Sneed, J.D. Souther, Fred Tackett,
Maxine Willard Waters
Recorded at Sunset Sound Recorders, Hollywood, 1976-1979
Producer: Lowell George
Release date: US: 23 March 1979
Peak position: US: 71
Running time: 31:25; CD reissue: 33:53

Just before Little Feat started work on *The Last Record Album* in 1975, Warner
Bros. – pleased with the success of *Feats Don't Fail Me Now* – renegotiated
the band's contract. The label's most prominent ask was a solo record from
George – as a buffer in case the band broke up. In return, the band and
their management got a $1,000,000 advance: the six band members getting
$100,000 each, and management getting the rest.

But the band needn't have worried about their leader running off to be a
solo star. He wasn't in a rush and finally started working on the album in 1976,
only because he figured it was about time. Even at the initial solo sessions –
all of which involved Little Feat – he only mustered enough interest to record
some demos for Valerie Carter's *Just a Stone's Throw Away*. Work on George's
solo album progressed intermittently over the next two and a half years,
with the majority of sessions taking place concurrently with the *Waiting for
Columbus* mixing.

Concerns that George was hoarding his best material for his solo project
were also unfounded, with Payne's frustration at George's detachment during
the *Time Loves a Hero* sessions, later assuaged, not only by how long it took
him to record the solo album, but by its dearth of original songs. George had

reached terminal decline and was more interested in extracurricular proclivities than completing his solo album. A much-needed distraction came with the tour promoting *Waiting for Columbus*, which started on 30 March 1978 and lasted well into the summer. But it was soon obvious that George – as he'd recently sang – had one foot on the platform and the other on the train. His interest simply wasn't there anymore, and at the end of the tour, instead of capitalizing on the live album's success and recording their sorely-overdue breakthrough album, George went off to produce the Grateful Dead's *Shakedown Street*.

But George didn't see *Shakedown Street* through to completion and wouldn't complete work on the album. Instead, he finally made good on his promise to Warner Bros., and finished his solo album. By late 1978, he had a collection of songs from a variety of sessions and musicians. True to form, he couldn't remember who played on what, and in his rambling liner notes, he simply rattled off a list of names, leaving the listener to figure it out.

The final sessions ran concurrently with Little Feat's in-progress *Down on the Farm*, and while George was initially able to divide his attention between both, his frustrations with Payne and Barrère (and theirs with him) reached breaking point. Fred Tackett, who worked closely with George on both the solo project and Little Feat's new album, recalled an enthusiastic George telling him, 'These guys have fired me. Help me put together a band for the solo project.' Tackett simply drafted in the musicians he'd been working with – Armando Compean, bass; Maxine Dixon, backing vocals; Don Heffington, drums; Jerry Jumonville, saxophone; Lee Thornberg, trumpet; Peter Wasner, keyboards, and Eddie Zip on organ. Tackett told Bud Scoppa in the *Hotcakes and Outtakes* liner notes: 'We went on the road, and the shows were great, and so were the reviews. This band was real raw, not heavy like Little Feat, and quieter. Lowell really liked it because he could sing without throwing his voice out every night.'

Indeed, *Thanks, I'll Eat It Here* (adapted from the second album's more ebullient working title *Thank You! I Will Eat It Here!*) has some of George's best vocals. But that was seemingly all the enthusiasm anyone could muster – especially George, who found his singing successful, later explaining to the *Boston Globe* that 'I was trying to sing and develop a style.' George's widow Liz confirmed his newfound focus on his method, telling Mark Brend in *Rock and Roll Doctor*: 'He did spend a lot of time during that period practicing his singing.'

But where were the songs? Of the nine, only 'Two Trains' and '20 Million Things' were solo George compositions, the former a remake of an old Little Feat track, the latter co-credited to his stepson Jed for coining the title line. He co-wrote only two others: 'Honest Man' and 'Cheek To Cheek.' The remainder were covers. George sheepishly shrugged this off in advance, telling *Rolling Stone*: 'I never seem to have the time to [write songs] anymore, at least not the way I'd like.'

This only furthers the idea that *Thanks, I'll Eat It Here* was a contractual obligation: a hodgepodge of songs collected to appease Warner Bros.

Right: Little Feat, 1976, clockwise from top left: Lowell George, Kenny Gradney, Paul Barrère, Richie Hayward, Sam Clayton, and Bill Payne. (*Pictoral Press/Alamy*)

Left: Showing off their not-so-little feet! Little Fox Theatre, Atlanta GA, 23 May 1975. (*Warner Bros. Records*)

Left: Little Feat's debut record album, an eccentric collection of songs that sold only about 11,000 copies. (*Warner Bros. Records*)

Left: *Sailin' Shoes*, despite being a perfect representation of early Little Feat, didn't do much better. (*Warner Bros. Records*)

Right: *Dixie Chicken* saw the line-up expand to six and introduced the 'Feats Auxiliary'. (*Warner Bros. Records*)

Right: George called *Feats Don't Fail Me Now* a 'party record – have a beer or two and dance'. (*Warner Bros. Records*)

Above: In full flight at the Tower Theatre, Upper Darby PA, 14 May 1977 (*georg w. purvis III*)

Right: George displays his unique bottleneck technique, 11/16' Craftsman spark plug socket and all. (*georg w. purvis III*)

Left: 'Roll right through the night': engaging in a bit of call-and-answer with the crowd. (*georg w. purvis III*)

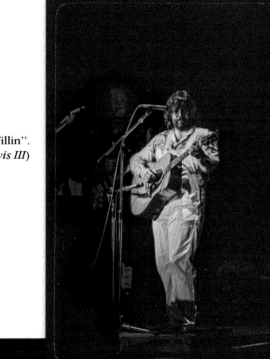

Right: George, still 'Willin''.
(*georg w. purvis III*)

Left: Gradney and Clayton, the shot in the arm Little Feat needed in 1972. (*georg w. purvis III*)

Left: 'Hollywood is nothing but a fruit dessert with Cool Whip': the cracks started to show on *The Last Record Album*. (*Warner Bros. Records*)

Left: With a disengaged leader, the others had to step up for the slick *Time Loves A Hero*. (*Warner Bros. Records*)

Right: The old Little Feat magic reappeared for the classic live record album *Waiting For Columbus*. (*Warner Bros. Records*)

Right: George's long-delayed solo album *Thanks, I'll Eat It Here* was released during a tumultuous period in Little Feat history. (*Warner Bros. Records*)

Left: Little Feat (with Emmylou Harris) hosted a superb episode of *Midnight Special* on 10 June 1977.

Right: Clayton at the Pinkpop Festival in Landgraaf, Netherlands, 7 June 1976.

Left: Hayward in the middle of a drum break during 'Rock and Roll Doctor' at Pinkpop.

Right: George slides down the neck of his guitar at Pinkpop.

Left: Trying to get the Dutch audience to sing along at Pinkpop.

Right: Barrère 'had a command of the blues that floored me' – Payne.

Left: Completed after George's death, *Down On The Farm* is a true labor of love from the surviving band members. (*Warner Bros. Records*)

Left: Payne and Barrère compiled *Hoy-Hoy!* to not only celebrate Little Feat but to also pay tribute to George. (*Warner Bros. Records*)

Right: Little Feat reformed in 1988 with Craig Fuller and released the excellent *Let It Roll*. (*Warner Bros. Records*)

Right: *Representing The Mambo*, a hidden gem, was too adventurous for mainstream radio. (*Warner Bros. Records*)

Left: Fuller's last record album with Little Feat, *Shake Me Up*, before leaving to spend more time with his family. (*Morgan Creek Records*)

Right: Shaun Murphy gave the band a much needed freshening up on *Ain't Had Enough Fun*. (*Zoo Entertainment*)

Left: 'Kinda how it's been for Little Feat...flyin' fast and low': the underappreciated *Under the Radar*. (*CMC International Records*)

Right: *Chinese Work Songs* was released during the height of the band's word-of-mouth grassroots campaign. (*CMC International Records*)

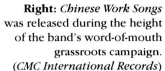

Left: *Kickin' It At The Barn*, their first studio record album on their own label. (*Hot Tomato Records*)

Right: Jimmy Buffett and others joined the band for this enjoyable celebration of Little Feat's past. (*Proper Records Ltd*)

Above: Though down two long-time members, Little Feat is still going strong at the Portland State Theatre, 21 November 2021.

Right: Scott Sharrard, who stepped in temporarily for an ailing Barrère in 2019, is now a full-time member.

Left: Payne, the only founding Feat left, keeps a watchful eye on the band.

Above: Onstage with the leg lamp from the 1983 holiday movie *A Christmas Story* between Clayton and Gradney.

Left: Fred Tackett was a long-time member of the 'Feats Auxiliary' before finally becoming a full-time Feat in 1988.

Right: Clayton's brother Joe was Aretha Franklin and Marvin Gaye's percussionist, and sister Merry duetted with Mick Jagger on 'Gimme Shelter'.

Left: *Rooster Rag* was the last studio record album to be released in Barrère's lifetime. (*Rounder Records*)

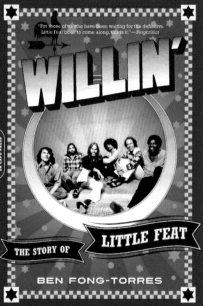

Right: Ben Fong-Torres' *Willin'* is *the* definitive biography on Little Feat. (*Da Capo Press*)

Left: Gabe Ford left, replaced Hayward after his death and stayed with the band until 2020. (*Ashley Stagg/Little Feat*)

Contemporary reviewers saw through the ruse, with *Sounds* calling it 'a pleasant diversion', and *Rolling Stone* lamenting that it 'isn't exactly the cornucopia of new Lowell George songs that Little Feat fans had been anticipating.' The album stalled at 71 in the US, and was a no-show in the UK. The singles 'What Do You Want The Girl To Do?' (US) and 'Cheek To Cheek' (UK) also failed to ignite any sales.

Warner Bros. requested a 21-date solo tour, which George agreed to, but it had been whittled down considerably by the time he hit the road on 15 June 1979. The band Tackett assembled, challenged George in a way that Little Feat hadn't. The band allowed the songs' subtlety and nuance to shine, allowing George to focus on his singing: something he couldn't do previously as he was constantly fighting against Little Feat's sheer sonic din.

George also readily spoke to the press: something he'd avoided previously. An especially chatty George discussed audience reactions and concert/album reviews with journalists while musing aloud on Little Feat's future, solo endeavors, and his desire to set up his own mobile studio and branch out further into production.

But George was overworked and perpetually under the weather. He'd ballooned to over 300 pounds and struggled to keep up, though this didn't hinder his cocaine consumption. His wife Liz joined him on tour, out of necessity, to keep his partying under control. But she maintained that he wanted to change, later telling Ben Fong-Torres:

I was always concerned about his health, to the point that it got to be 'Can we do this anymore? If you don't care, how can I care?' I mean, I didn't give up, but … the day before he died, we had a conversation, and he said, 'I know I need help, and when I get home, I will get help.' Because I said that was required. And home he never got.

On the night of 28 June, after a triumphant return to Lisner Auditorium, George attended a post-show party until the small hours. When that came to an end, he met up with road manager Gene Vano to work on an upcoming *King Biscuit Flower Hour* radio broadcast, though Vano eventually went to a coffee shop for a break. A few minutes after returning to his room, Liz frantically knocked on his door, after being unable to rouse her husband. Vano was able to turn him over and get him breathing, but it didn't last. 20 minutes later, the paramedics were called and George was transferred to Arlington Hospital, where – after 1:00 p.m. – he was announced as dead of a massive heart attack. He was 34 years old.

George's former bandmates were shocked, if not surprised. Barrère described himself as 'emotionally devastated,' while Hayward – laid up in traction after another motorcycle accident – said he 'felt robbed. I wasn't even able to play the memorial concert for Lowell.' Gradney and Clayton were both unable to process the news at first, and Payne went into survival mode:

'My first thought – other than anger, then sadness – was 'Did he cover his kids, insurance-wise?' Hayward later recalled to Bud Scoppa: 'I called up the accountants and asked them, and they said he didn't. So I called up Ronstadt and a couple of other people, and we put together a benefit and memorial to Lowell: a tribute.'

Payne threw his energy into organizing the concert, serving as musical director, while Barrère was the master of ceremonies. A wide cast of friends, family and people who'd worked with George, helped out. Linda Ronstadt, Jackson Browne, Emmylou Harris, Nicolette Larson, Michael McDonald, Patrick Simmons, Bonnie Raitt and Tower of Power all showed up, with the Hayward-less Feats augmented by drummer Rick Shlosser, bassist Bob Glaub, percussionist Bobby LaKind, Fred Tackett and Craig Fuller on guitar and vocals, Ted Templeman on percussion, and saxophonist Jerry Jumonville. It was a wild party, raising $230,000 for George's family. Liz later told Fong-Torres: 'It was a wonderful celebration of the man and his music, and it was very helpful to the family. Was a long time coming to grips with mourning and moving on, for me.'

George's former bandmates agreed, with Barrère telling the same interviewer: 'At the very tail-end of it when we were all in the dressing room, I just kinda broke down, we gave each other a hug ... It just was draining.' Untethered by George's incalculable absence, the rest of Little Feat would struggle to escape the shadow of their beloved leader. But there was still one last album to finish.

'What Do You Want the Girl to Do' (Allen Toussaint)
US A-side (WBS-8847), May 1979

George takes another stab at an Allen Toussaint track, this time transforming the soul highlight of Toussaint's 1975 album *Southern Nights* into a gentle disco-fied stomper. While George undoubtedly improved the arrangement – with a tight rhythm section and warm horns – it was perhaps a little *too* contemporary, with the sultry backing vocals and string synthesizer especially dating it now. It was the album's sole US single (b/w '20 Million Things'), predictably failing to chart. But it did earn a spot in George's solo repertoire.

'Honest Man' (Lowell George, Fred Tackett)
UK B-side (K-17379), July 1979

This is the first released collaboration between Lowell George and Fred Tackett (one further co-write, 'Be Here Now' ended up on *Down On the Farm*). Unfortunately, the track plods and struggles to ignite interest. The song was played on George's solo tour, and was also performed by the reformed Feat – with Tackett now a full-time member – but not until the end of 1996, after which it became a setlist staple.

'Two Trains' (Lowell George)

George recasts 'Two Trains' as a jittery funk piece, with the arrangement (finally) allowing for gritty guitar and even a lick of bottleneck, along with drum embellishments. The biggest surprise is the complete rewrite of the verses (the choruses are mostly unchanged). Instead of pondering infidelity, now he's waiting for – and then riding – a train. While George was notorious for never letting a song sit still for too long – always finding something to refine – he rarely changed the lyrics once they were established. In this case, one wishes he'd left well enough alone.

'I Can't Stand The Rain' (Ann Peebles, Don Bryant, Bernie Miller)

Renowned for its studio trickery (electric timbales emulating raindrops) as much as its superb vocal and arrangement, this was Ann Peebles' signature song, not to mention her most successful: 38 in the US pop charts, 6 R&B, and 41 in the UK.

George had always wanted to record the song, and perhaps recognizing its status, wisely stuck close to the original arrangement: thus justifying the horn section and whichever of the nine credited drummers smacked the timbales. Though he couldn't help but shoehorn in a lovely slide guitar solo.

'Cheek To Cheek' (Lowell George, Van Dyke Parks, Martin Kibbee)

UK A-side (K-17379), July 1979

Side two opens with this mariachi pastiche, George adapting a vaguely Mexican inflection as he sings of drinking too much tequila and falling in love on Rosarito Beach. A marked shift from side one's light disco and blue-eyed soul leanings, this was viewed as a novelty (Its choice as the sole UK single was a questionable one), though George maintained his appreciation for the genre, and credited Van Dyke Parks for introducing him to the music of influential singer/songwriter Miguel Aceves Mejía.

'Easy Money' (Rickie Lee Jones)

One of George's many natural talents was discovering and nurturing those of others: Bonnie Raitt, Valerie Carter, Tret Fure and Linda Ronstadt were all taken under his wing, and benefited his tutelage. One of his final protégées was Rickie Lee Jones: a Chicago-born singer/songwriter living in Los Angeles who met George through their mutual friend Ivan Ulz. Smitten by her song 'Easy Money,' George immediately called Jones up to record the song for his album.

While he did stake his claim on the song, he also helped Jones secure a record deal with Warner Bros. Lenny Waronker and Russ Titelman produced her eponymous debut album, and – assisted by her smash debut single 'Chuck E.'s in Love' – it soared to number 3 in February 1979. The following month, George's solo album came out, including his faithful interpretation of 'Easy Money.' Compared to Jones' cooler, more jazz-like approach, George's rendition is a little more boogied up, with a steady backbeat, punchy horns and even a short slide guitar solo.

'20 Million Things' (Lowell George, Jed Levy)
US B-side (WBS-8847), May 1979

George delivers a knockout with this gentle country/soul ballad. It was inspired by his eight-year-old stepson Jed, who'd been gifted a tape recorder for Christmas and found entertainment in babbling and singing into it with his friends. George's ears pricked up when he heard Jed utter, 'I've got twenty million things to do, but I'm only thinking of you.' Using that line as a starting point, he came up with a procrastinator's anthem, and gave Jed a well-deserved credit.

Recorded at Sunset Sound Recorders on 21 October 1977 and featuring Fred Tackett and Dean Parks on acoustic guitar (and possibly Jeff Porcaro on drums), '20 Million Things' remains an obscure classic, tucked away on side two. It slipped out as the US B-side to 'What Do You Want the Girl to Do' but was never performed live. It also appeared on the expanded 1993 *As Time Goes By* compilation and the 2000 *Hotcakes and Outtakes* box set.

'Find A River' (Fred Tackett)
Singer/songwriter and Feats Auxiliary member Fred Tackett had been promoted to collaborator and musical director for the album, so it's no surprise that – as he had with 'Fool Yourself' on 1973's *Dixie Chicken* – George recorded another Tackett song. This is a sublime ballad, starting with George's voice and Tackett's acoustic guitar, though the arrangement builds in intensity, with a shimmering electric piano and deeply-tuned drums. It's a lovely companion-piece to the similar '20 Million Things', but isn't one of the album's better-known songs – Tackett attempted to rectify this in 2003, by recording a version on his debut solo album *In a Town Like This*, which also included a recording of 'Honest Man.'

'Himmler's Ring' (Jimmy Webb)
Songwriter Jimmy Webb had introduced George to Fred Tackett, both of whom would hang out at Webb's mansion in the late-1960s, thus kick-starting a brief but rewarding friendship and collaborative partnership between George and Tackett. While Webb's best-known song was 'MacArthur Park' (which George couldn't stand), it was his more eccentric songs that delighted George, so he paid homage by closing *Thanks, I'll Eat It Here* with Webb's 'Himmler's Ring.'

George delights in the arrangement, with its boozy brass, woozy violin and brushed drums reminiscent of the music hall, while the instrumental break is a nice reference to the subject matter. Because of its unconventional instrumentation and arrangement for the time, 'Himmler's Ring' doesn't have many admirers, with Webb even admitting to *The San Diego Union-Tribune* in

2017 that it 'was a kind of a barbed-wire affair with 'Himmler's Ring,' which I think was widely misunderstood by most people. It was a satire of a guy who collects Nazi war memorabilia. I thought that was a singular hook for a song.'

Still, it's a boatload of fun and serves as an eccentric conclusion to an eccentric album that jumps around the musical landscape. Given George's appreciation for such unconventional genres and styles, it would've been fascinating to see what avenues he might've explored with the eventual popularity of world music in the late-1980s.

Related Tracks
'Heartache' (Lowell George, Ivan Ulz)
This recording of the Ivan Ulz co-write for Valerie Carter's *Just a Stone's Throw Away* album is George's original acoustic demo from 1976. Carter added backing vocals much later for its appearance on the 1993 CD reissue of *Thanks, I'll Eat It Here*. While it's not surprising that the song didn't make the original album (Had it been a contender, it would've likely been adorned with additional instrumentation), any previously unknown Lowell George recording is always welcome.

Down on the Farm (1979)

Personnel:
Paul Barrère: guitar, vocals; lead vocal on 'Down On The Farm'
Sam Clayton: congas, vocals; lead vocal on 'Feel The Groove'
Lowell George: vocals, guitar
Kenny Gradney: bass
Richie Hayward: drums, vocals
Bill Payne: keyboards, synthesizer, vocals; lead vocal on 'Wake Up Dreaming'
Additional personnel:
Fred Tackett: electronic aids, guitar solo on 'Kokomo'
David Lindley: electronic aids, slide guitar
'Sneaky' Pete Kleinow: electronic aids, pedal steel guitar
Robben Ford: wonder thunder, guitar
Gordon DeWitty: keyboards on 'Feel The Groove'
Earl Palmer: drums on 'Feel The Groove'
Rosemary Butler, Bonnie Raitt, Dan Smith, Fran Tate, Julia Waters, Luther Waters, Oren Waters, and Maxine Willard Waters: backing vocals
Jerry Jumonville: saxophone
Lee Thornburg: trumpet, trombone
Recorded at Paramount Ranch, Agoura Hills, and Lowell's house, Topanga Canyon, with the Wally Heider Mobile Truck, January-April 1979; Wally Heider Recording, Hollywood, August-September 1979
Producer: Lowell George... with a little help from his friends
Release date: US: 14 November 1979
Peak position: US: 29, UK: 46
Running time: 36:22

After *Waiting for Columbus*, Little Feat found themselves in a predicament: they now had a hit live album to promote, yet the only way to promote it was to go back out on the road. They were set to start on 7 March 1978 with a brief Japanese tour (their first ever), but a motorcycle accident had other plans. This time it was George who took a spill – while goofing around on his bike in the dirt, he attempted one too many wheelies and was thrown clear over the handlebars, rupturing several vertebral discs and losing sensation in his left hand. An operation was required. George feared he would be out of commission for too long, but, as he told T. E. Mattox of Tokyo's Armed Forces Radio on 7 July, his surgeon 'realized that I was a musician, and made a real concerted effort to revive the nerves that had stopped in my hand. 'Cause I couldn't play the guitar anymore. And I have to say, only when I get tense does it bother me at all. And it's mostly just minor pain in my back. I went back to work two weeks later.'

    With the Japanese dates postponed until 1 July, on 30 March, the band started a lengthy 52-date North American tour in Detroit, ending nearly three months later on 18 June in Hollywood. Band relations had improved somewhat, and George was more engaged than previously (even if he still left the stage for 'Day At The Dog Races'). There was even a glimmer of the former camaraderie – with George often introducing Payne as Knuckles for his 'Willin'' piano solo, Barrère as 'the other guitar player,' and Barrère introducing George as 'the Pillsbury Doughboy of rock and roll.' But the bonhomie didn't last long. While George finally seemed determined to wrest back control of Little Feat by suggesting they record a live album, none of the interpersonal issues had been addressed, so the tension still bubbled beneath the surface. It also didn't help that George had no interest in returning to the studio with the band. Instead, he started production on the Grateful Dead's *Shakedown Street*, but failed to finish his work by the time of Little Feat's autumn tour, and so had to bow out. But another Little Feat album was due, so in the new year, they duly assembled to begin recording.

This time, instead of recording in the stifling studio confines, George wanted to record in a more comfortable, relaxed environment, like his house. Pilfering the recording method he'd used for the Dead, George set up Wally Heider's mobile recording truck at the Paramount Ranch in Agoura Hills, to lay down rhythm tracks before moving the truck to his house in Topanga Canyon to record vocals.

Payne wasn't thrilled with the arrangement. He told Bud Scoppa:

Whether it was a mess or not, I perceived it to be. I would walk out into the main room, and there would be a microphone not even close to the amp. There wasn't a real room sound there that I recall. Nobody was paying attention. That just drove me completely over the edge … I kept thinking, 'What are we doing? We deserve better than this.'

After voicing his concerns to George, Payne asked if he could get involved in the production. He recalled to Ben Fong-Torres: 'He told me flat out 'No,' and I went, 'Well, if that's the answer, then screw it, I don't really want to do this' … I was pissed off.'

Whether he was pissed off enough to quit the band or just take a breather, Payne's next step was to go out on the road with Fran and Barrère as part of Nicolette Larson's band. George was apoplectic: now tasked with finishing the album on his own, he took every opportunity he could to denigrate Payne in the press. George snapped at *NME*'s Peter Erskine: 'I must admit I got pretty tired of everybody … seeing me as some kind of ogre. For years now, they've seen me as an ogre.' He was also furious at Payne and Barrère for 'bad-rapping me to people in the record company for what they have called my 'excessive behavior.''

There was probably some confusion as to who was actually in the band or if there was even a band at all. Payne had suggested that the band take a break and explore other outlets before getting back together, to which George was receptive. But when Payne said he and Barrère 'were looking at other people to play with,' George flipped the script and insisted he'd been fired from Little Feat. But even *he* couldn't stick to that story for too long, complaining to WHCN DJ Ed O'Connell that Payne had betrayed him by quitting: 'It was about two-thirds done when Bill Payne came in and went, 'I quit.' Which was really a big help, which really did a lot to my ego ... He said, 'If things don't get better after this record's done, I'm going to quit.' And he went back on his word and quit right in the midst of it. And I have to say, that really got to me.'

Work on the album ended by April, as George's solo debut had been released and he had to prepare for a brief solo tour. As far as he was concerned, this tour was more of a distraction than a mission statement, and he was determined to finish *Down on the Farm*, booking studio time for later in the summer. He would never return.

After George's memorial concert at The Forum on 4 August, Little Feat reassembled at Wally Heider Recording in Hollywood to put the finishing touches on the unfinished album. Due to the ramshackle early sessions, there was concern there might not be enough material for a full album. Reviewing the existing tapes, there were enough usable backing tracks, but a considerable amount of work was needed to make the songs releasable.

Luckily, George had recorded vocals for the songs he'd decided to sing, but they were rough takes. Considering that was all they had to work with, the result is impressive, but a noticeable step down in quality from the vocal heights he'd reached on his solo album. Unfortunately, he hadn't recorded as many guitar parts, and what *was* recorded was so rough that most of his parts couldn't be used. Payne recruited Fred Tackett to tap into the directions George might've been aiming for on his solos. In many cases, Tackett complemented George's original lines using his guitar and amplifier. But further enhancements were needed – as a result, David Lindley and 'Sneaky' Pete Kleinow were credited with 'electronic aids' and Robben Ford with 'wonder thunder.'

There were other guest musicians, too – Sam Clayton's 'Feel The Groove' featured its co-writer and arranger Gordon DeWitty on keyboards, with legendary drummer Earl Palmer deputizing for Hayward (laid up from a motorcycle accident). Eight backing vocalists (including Bonnie Raitt and Payne's wife Fran) helped where they were needed.

By the time of the album's November release, Little Feat (and Lowell George) were effectively *persona non grata* in both the hit parade (29 in the US – albeit a Little Feat studio album career-high – and 46 in the UK) and the music press. *Rolling Stone* didn't care enough to even publish a review. In *The Washington Post,* John Rabb wrote that the album 'stands as a requiem for George, and for the kind of music the group made together for almost ten years,' but that 'It's a shame that – for the life they led – Little Feat must go out with a relative whimper instead of a bang. Sad to say, but *Down on the Farm* is just not up to snuff, even for a band to whom lapses-in-inspiration were commonplace. When the album shines, as it infrequently does, it is often because of George's contributions.'

The *New York Times'* Robert Palmer found it 'a pleasant surprise to find that while *Down on the Farm* is a little schizophrenic, on the whole, it's the kind of album Mr. George probably would have wanted it to be ... For the most part, *Down on the Farm* does the band proud.'

With the now-customary absurdist Neon Park cover – this time showing a se-duck-tress painting her nails poolside while a tiger looks on behind her (The album's original title was *Duck Lips*) – and rambling George-esque liner notes, *Down on the Farm* (described as 'the real last record album' in the liner notes) serves as a sufficient if unremarkable conclusion to a band who deserved so much more. Barrère found the recording process to be an emotionally-draining labor of love, telling *Rolling Stone*: 'The band finished this album for Lowell, and because of that, it's probably gonna sound more like a group project than if Lowell were still alive.' Payne agreed: 'It's not a perfect album, but the stuff he did is ... great. There are cuts, too, that will bridge that personal feeling about Lowell George. And I'm quite anxious for people to hear that it's not a jazz-blues album at all. In fact, there are so many styles, that this album is almost a revamp of *Sailin' Shoes*.'

As for the future of Little Feat, Barrère and Payne were blunt: there wasn't one. The guitarist told *Rolling Stone*: 'Whatever doors were open to anymore Little Feat albums, are now closed'; the keyboardist simply adding, 'Little Feat just does not exist without Lowell.'

Famous last words.

'Down On The Farm' (Paul Barrère, Gabriel Barrère)

Opening with some *audio vérité* of George arguing with a persistently-ribbiting frog, this is a joyful boogie rocker, harkening back to the woozy, boozy days of *Sailin' Shoes* and *Dixie Chicken*. Heavily inspired by the Meters song 'They All Ask'd for You,' 'Down On The Farm' takes on a more poignant tone in light of George's passing – especially lines like 'Miss you so much that crying's all we can do/Weeping and wailing, praying you'll come home soon'. Written on the page, it's almost touching, but when delivered with Barrère's tongue-in-cheek drawl, the listener can be forgiven for believing that even the farm animals were grieving George's death. Well, stranger things have happened!

'Six Feet Of Snow' (Lowell George, Keith Godchaux)

This was written with Grateful Dead keyboardist Keith Godchaux during sessions for their *Shakedown Street* album. George's vocal is the perfect combination of soulful and weary, due to it being a rough, yet it works in this situation, as the song was borne from the loneliness of the road: 'Six feet of snow comin' through my radio/It's rainin' in stilettos from here clear down to Mexico.' Unlike other road songs – inevitably inspired by the touring musician's lifestyle – George once again tapped into the inner psyche of a long-haul trucker: his hands numb from clutching the steering wheel, dreaming of his girl back home in New Orleans.

'Perfect Imperfection' (Paul Barrère, Tom Snow)

Though it has a slick, jazz-like smoothness that would've more suited the previous two albums, this is nevertheless one of this album's highlights, and is a superb testament to Barrère's mature songwriting. Co-writer Tom Snow is an established songwriter who in 1979 had already written hits for Gayle McCormick, Olivia Newton-John, Rita Coolidge and others. Barrère would collaborate with Snow again: on the song 'Who Knows For Sure' on his first post-Feats album *On My Own Two Feet*.

Unusually, George takes the lead vocal here, and by Barrère's admission, it was only meant to a rough vocal, but it turned out 'great. And then we brought in Bonnie to add some background vocals … and it was sweet.'

'Kokomo' (Lowell George)

Another slight funk-rocker, this is George's only solo songwriting credit on the album, and recalls the mid-paced boogie rock of 'Two Trains': which he'd recently updated for his solo album, though it isn't one of his better songs. At least he had fun with the lyrics – singing of a girl ('Miss Demeanour') who 'smells so sweet like apple pie' and that 'For a slice or two, I'd be a fool.'

'Be One Now' (Lowell George, Fred Tackett)

Written in late-1978 at the start of the album sessions, this is not only the album highlight, but a forgotten latter-day classic on a par with 'Long Distance Love' and 'Mercenary Territory.' The mid-tempo pop ballad's production is a little soft, but George's vocal, despite being a rough take, is superb. The song certainly deserves wider recognition than being tucked away on Little Feat's posthumous last record album.

'Straight From The Heart' (Lowell George, Bill Payne)

This was the first genuine George/Payne co-write since 1973's 'Lafayette Railroad,' and is a pleasantly funky yet poppy arrangement. George sounds fully engaged here, singing with a passion and enthusiasm that suggest this might've been one of the songs he considered closest to completion in his lifetime; even the bottleneck guitar sounds like George, though Barrère later told Ben Fong-Torres that 'the slide that I did on 'Straight From The Heart,' Billy kind of coached me through it because he wanted a dual slide part with a kind of harmony to it.'

'Front Page News' (Lowell George, Bill Payne)

US B-side (WBS-49169), 23 January 1980

Another perpetual 'maybe next time' since 1974, this song was finally given a fair shake, with George now given a co-credit (Payne would be credited as sole writer on the earlier recordings on *Hoy-Hoy!* and *Hotcakes and Outtakes*).

George favored this particular arrangement, which calls into question his criticism of Payne's jazz-fusion leanings. George's vocal is especially impassioned, and Barrère – who wasn't even around for the recording – later heaped praise on the song: 'That whole track knocks my socks off.'

An edit (4:21) was released as the B-side of an equally-edited 'Wake Up Dreaming' in January 1980. 'Front Page News' was also known to be performed once in 1973: at the band's second gig without Hayward, who George had sacked and replaced with Fred White.

'Wake Up Dreaming' (Bill Payne, Fran Payne)
US A-side (WBS-49169), 23 January 1980

Payne's third Feats co-write with his wife Fran was probably the most conventional. It's a light but slick, radio-friendly rocker sounding closer to the Doobie Brothers.music of the day than Little Feat. But it's still a decent song, with some deft Robben Ford guitar work. It's unlikely George contributed to this song or even knew that it existed.

Warner Bros. decided it had the most potential chart success, issuing an edited (3:40) single in January 1980 b/w 'Front Page News,' but, predictably, it failed to chart.

'Feel The Groove' (Sam Clayton, Gordon DeWitty; Arranged by Gordon DeWitty)
This funky piece was instigated and sung by Sam Clayton at George's insistence. While the lyrics don't say much, and the track overstays its welcome (it would've been a better side-one closer), Clayton's carefree, breezy vocal, DeWitty's groovy funk and the simmering backing track make it a worthwhile inclusion.

Related Tracks
'Boogie Wigwam (Short Jazz Piece)' (Bill Payne)
Recorded in January 1979 at the Paramount Ranch in Agoura Hills, this lark (essentially Payne, Gradney and Hayward goofing around for 40 seconds) was obviously not considered as serious (punctuated by Payne's 'That's all folks!' finale) and was eventually released on *Hotcakes and Outtakes*, with the cryptic "'PZM' Pressure Mic' demo-qualifier added. ('PZM' stands for 'Pressure Zone Microphone': a condenser microphone, so it's likely this recording was captured on one.)

Hoy-Hoy! (1981)

Personnel:
Paul Barrère: guitar, vocals
Sam Clayton: congas, percussion, vocals
Lowell George: vocals, guitars
Kenny Gradney: bass
Richie Hayward: drums, percussion, vocals
Bill Payne: piano, organ, keyboards, vocals
Additional recording information noted after individual songs.
Producers: Bill Payne, George Massenburg and Paul Barrère; 'Forty-Four Blues'
and 'Strawberry Flats' produced by Russ Titelman; 'Easy To Slip' produced by Ted
Templeman
Release date: US: 29 July 1981
Peak position: US: 39, UK: 76
Running time: 69:34

Down on the Farm had been an emotional struggle from start to finish,
and while it took each band member a considerable amount of fortitude to
complete, the result was surprisingly strong. Still, Payne didn't think it ended
the story properly, telling Mary Turner in 1984 that he wanted to release
something 'to give everybody who was interested, a little more insight into
what this group was about.' In 1980, Payne approached Warner Bros. chairman
Mo Ostin with the idea of a final Little Feat album – he didn't need much
convincing.

Aided and abetted by George Massenburg, Payne's vision was not to present
the *greatest hits* (They didn't have any), but to offer a cross-section of what
Little Feat were about throughout their existence. That meant including mostly
familiar tracks in unfamiliar formats: demos, live recordings, radio broadcasts
and outtakes. The compilation was rounded off with a trio of previously released
songs as a flashback to early Feats, and two new recordings for good measure.

Hoy-Hoy! is a celebration of Little Feat and a tribute to Lowell George, who
appears on all but three songs. Other band members come and go, but George
is the focus – though, in the liner notes, very little attempt is made to glamorize
the way he lived (and died). Nearly everyone in the Feats saga gets to say
their piece (Hayward's contribution was doodles and illustrations), including
Massenburg, Van Dyke Parks, Martin Kibbee, Bonnie Raitt, road managers Rick
Harper and Gene Vano, and George's widow Elizabeth.

The packaging is like a scrapbook, with band photos, liner notes, collages
by George, Neon Park artwork and concert reviews – in Japanese and German.
The cover was adapted from artwork Park did for an early-1970s calendar
– infamously used as the cover image for the *Electrif Lycanthrope* bootleg –
reworked and colorised. As for the title, the official Little Feat website offers
a few reasons, the most logical being a reference to Alexander Graham Bell's
preferred greeting when answering a telephone, though taken as a reference

to Howlin' Wolf's 'Three Hundred Pounds of Joy' – 'Hoy! Hoy! I'm the boy' – it's a neat flashback to the bluesman most influential on Lowell George. The phrase also graced George Washington and Marilyn Monroe's Cadillac license plate on the *Feats Don't Fail Me Now* cover image (the translation from Spanish to English being the rather mundane 'Today! Today!'). It also popped up consistently throughout Park's artwork, so it's really just a long-running inside joke.

Released in July 1981, *Hoy-Hoy!* gave Little Feat a US top-40 album, but it was a disappointing flop in the UK. The music press were either conciliatory – '*Hoy-Hoy!* intends to be affectionate, not definitive, not a last gasp, but, in the Little Feat tradition, a last laugh' (Jon Pareles, *Rolling Stone*) – or contentious: '*Hoy-Hoy!* is a great disservice and not at all indicative of the band's excellence or the diversity of its material,' *The Washington Post*'s Richard Harrington opined. 'This is the kind of record a company puts out when they've lost an act, not when they're trying to honor it.'

It didn't matter to Payne – he'd achieved what he set out to do by providing a suitable epitaph for a band that should've been more recognized and renowned. What he didn't know was that his next move would (briefly) achieve just that.

'Rocket In My Pocket' (Lowell George demo) (Lowell George)
Recorded at Saddle Peak Studios, 1978

This demo consists of George on guitar, vocal and rhythm box. He may have been considering an updated version for his solo album.

'Rock And Roll Doctor' (Alternate version) (Lowell George, Martin Kibbee)
Recorded live 1974-1976 for WLIR. Re-recorded at Blue Seas, Baltimore; RCA, New York; Sea-Saint Studio, New Orleans, and Sound Factory, West Los Angeles, until nothing survived. Allen Toussaint: backing vocal and horn arrangements.

Taking an electrifying Feats performance from 19 September 1974 at Ultrasound Studios, George asked legendary New Orleans composer Allen Toussaint to write backing vocal and horn arrangements (recorded at his Sea-Saint Studio). George then continued to tinker, having no specific destination for the track. Now that it lives on *Hoy-Hoy!*, it's nice to have an alternative to compare to the original.

'Skin It Back' (Live) (Paul Barrère)
Recorded at Lisner Auditorium, Washington, D.C., 8 August 1977. Barrère: vocal

The first of three *Waiting for Columbus* outtakes, this performance benefits tremendously from the Tower of Power horn section.

77

'Red Streamliner' (Live) (Bill Payne, Fran Tate)
Recorded at Lisner Auditorium, Washington, D.C., 8 August 1977. Payne: vocal; Michael McDonald and Patrick Simmons: backing vocals

Another *Columbus* outtake, this achieves greater heights than on *Time Loves a Hero,* thanks to George's slide work. Doobie Brothers Michael McDonald and Patrick Simmons stopped by Lisner to reprise their backing vocals.

'Lonesome Whistle' (Lowell George demo) (Hank Williams, Jimmie H. Davis)
Recorded at Blue Seas Recording Studio, Hunt Valley, 1974. Richie Hayward and Lee Lawler: backing vocals

Despite its credit as being recorded by 'Lowell hisself' and being intended for his solo album, this is almost certainly a Feats performance – Hayward is on backing vocals and drums, and that's unmistakably Payne on piano.

'Front Page News' (Original) (Bill Payne)
Recorded at Blue Seas Recording Studio, Hunt Valley, 1974. Payne: vocal; Emmylou Harris and Fran Tate: backing vocals. US B-side (WBS-49801), 5 August 1981

Finally released on *Down on the Farm* with a George co-write credit, this is the original arrangement from the *Feats Don't Fail Me Now* sessions.

'The Fan' (Live) (Lowell George, Bill Payne)
Recorded for WLIR at Ultrasonic Recording Studios, Hempstead, 19 September 1974

Like 'Rock And Roll Doctor,' this was recorded at Ultrasonic for WLIR, and was eventually liberated on the *Electrif Lycanthrope* bootleg.

'Teenage Nervous Breakdown' (Lowell George demo) (Lowell George)
Recorded at TTG, 1969. Elliott Ingber: guitar; Roy Estrada: bass; with 'more drummers than space to note them.'

Lasting less than 90 seconds, this post-The Factory/pre-Little Feat recording is drastically different from the *Sailin' Shoes* version. Just as it starts to get interesting, the song fades into…

'Teenage Nervous Breakdown' (Live) (Lowell George)
Recorded at Lisner Auditorium, Washington, D.C., 9 August 1977

…the third and final *Columbus* outtake – faster than the *Sailin' Shoes* version but twice as long, with Feats firing on all cylinders.

'Framed' (Jerry Lieber, Mike Stoller)
Recorded at TTG, 1969. Elliott Ingber: guitar; Roy Estrada: bass

Recorded at the same session as the 'Teenage Nervous Breakdown' demo, this cover of The Robins' (later The Coasters) 1954 single was part of a four-track demo for Frank Zappa's manager Herb Cohen: the only song of the four that would be recorded for a future Feats album.

'Gringo' (Bill Payne)
Recorded at The Complex, West Los Angeles, February 1981. Payne: vocal; Nicolette Larson, Fran Payne and Bobby LaKind: backing vocals; David Sanborn: saxophone; Robben Ford: acoustic guitar; Paulinho da Costa: percussion; Denny Yeager: Synclavier II programming. US A-side (WBS-49841), 23 September 1981

One of two new songs recorded for the album, 'Gringo' was inspired by a trip Payne took to Mexico in his 20s with road manager Rick Harper, and it's a towering achievement for Payne. It's doubtful George would've liked it – the song had its origins in the final tour's improvisational jazz-fusion moments in 'Day At The Dog Races.' Learning from George, Payne stored away some of those riffs, and returned to them for *Hoy-Hoy!*, constructing an impressive performance that hangs together well.

Recorded at the tail end of the production sessions, 'Gringo' is a fine ensemble performance where no one musician dominates, though each gets a chance to show their skills. Payne's keyboard-playing is deft and mature, his vocals arguably his finest to date, while Gradney and Clayton slink around Hayward's complicated patterns. (Barrère appears to be absent.) The band is rounded off by a small list of guest musicians, but it's David Sanborn's soaring saxophone that lifts the song to spectacular heights.

Warner Bros. released 'Gringo' as the second *Hoy-Hoy!* single: evidently undeterred that the 'Easy To Slip' reissue had stiffed in the charts. So too did 'Gringo,' despite it being stripped of three minutes to a more compact listen for the airwaves.

'Over The Edge' (Paul Barrère)
Recorded at the Complex, West Los Angeles, February 1981. Barrère: vocal and 'a thousand and one guitars'

This was Barrère's contribution to *Hoy-Hoy!*, written for the film of the same name at the request of his brother Robert: an editor on the film. Whether demoed and rejected or just not finished in time, Barrère never noted, but the song ultimately didn't make the soundtrack. Instead, Little Feat's 'All That You Dream' was included among tracks by Cheap Trick, The Cars, Van Halen, Ramones, and Valerie Carter.

Unlike 'Gringo,' this sounds derivative (don't be surprised if you feel compelled to sing 'Honky Tonk Women'), with a mix that buries Barrère's voice and obscures the lyrics. While this song might've been fine for Barrère's two post-Feats solo albums, it sits at odds with the rest of *Hoy-Hoy!*, and it's hard to believe this came from the same sessions as 'Gringo'. That said, it's not a bad song, as it taps into Barrère's state of mind at the time. Payne commented in the liner notes that the song was 'an anthem to what he was going through at the time.'

'Two Trains' (Live) (Lowell George)
Recorded at Ultrasonic Recording Studios, Hempstead, for WLIR, 10 April 1973

A rough-but-rollicking performance, this recording sticks fairly closely to the *Dixie Chicken* arrangement.

'China White' (Lowell George)
Recorded at Sunset Sound Recorders, Hollywood, 1978. Julia Waters, Luther Waters, Oren Waters, and Maxine Willard Waters: backing vocals; David Foster: piano; Dean Parks, Fred Tackett, guitar; Jim Keltner: drums; Chuck Rainey: bass; Gordon DeWitty: organ; Jerry Jumonville, Lee Thornburg: horns

While the subject matter – an ode to George's fondness for heroin ('I think it was probably rather easy for him to write, if you know what I mean,' his widow Elizabeth pointedly wrote in the *Hoy-Hoy!* liner notes) – might've felt a little too raw to have been released so soon after George's death, the performance more than justifies its inclusion. Starting off with George groaning away, accompanying himself on bottleneck, the song is reminiscent of 'Sailin' Shoes' or 'A Apolitical Blues.' But after verse one, it zigzags into a soulful, gospel-infused belter: each successive section building in intensity.

That the track was held from release for so long may seem like a tragedy, but it needed time to mature. The earliest available recording is from 1 April 1973, when Bonnie Raitt sang a harmony vocal with George in the late show at Paul's Mall in Boston. Feats played the song only six more times between 1973 and 1977, but George was never completely satisfied with their renditions. This recording – likely intended for *Thanks, I'll Eat It Here* – was also sadly deemed surplus to requirements.

'All That You Dream' (Live) (Paul Barrère, Bill Payne)
Recorded at the Lowell George Tribute Concert, The Forum, Inglewood, 4 August 1979. Linda Ronstadt: lead vocal; Nicolette Larson and Rosemary Butler: backing vocals; Rick Shlosser: drums; Bobby LaKind, Ted Templeman: percussion

This performance was a highlight of the memorial concert: Linda Ronstadt owns the song completely, though there's an obvious George-sized absence in the guitar department.

'Feets Don't Fail Me Now' (Live extract) (Paul Barrère, Lowell George, Martin Kibbee)
Recorded at the Tower Theatre, Upper Darby, 4 May 1976. The group and the entire city of Philadelphia: backing vocals

As the cheers from the *Fabulous Forum* fade out, the finale 'Feats Don't Fail Me Now' (for some reason using the anatomical spelling) fades in, the band assisted by a vociferous and enthusiastic crowd. It's a classy way to end the album and a suitable close to this particular Little Feat chapter.

Let It Roll (1988)

Personnel:
Paul Barrère: guitar, vocals; lead vocal on 'Let It Roll' and 'Business As Usual'; co-lead vocal on 'Hate To Lose Your Lovin'' and 'Cajun Girl'
Sam Clayton: percussion, vocals
Craig Fuller: vocals, button accordion, guitar
Kenny Gradney: bass
Richie Hayward: drums, vocals
Bill Payne: keyboards, vocals; co-lead vocal on 'Changin' Luck'
Fred Tackett: guitar, mandolin, trumpet
Additional personnel:
Renée Armand, Marilyn Martin, Shaun Murphy, Bonnie Raitt, Linda Ronstadt, Bob Seger: backing vocals
Recorded at The Complex, West Los Angeles, spring/summer 1988
Producers: George Massenburg, Bill Payne
Release date: US: 2 August 1988
Peak position: US: 36
Running time: 50:13

The Little Feat wilderness years began shortly after the release of *Hoy-Hoy!*. Payne stopped writing songs and dove into session work and touring (his marriage to Fran Tate had ended too); Hayward toured with Joan Armatrading and Robert Plant; Gradney joined Bob Weir's Bobby and the Midnights and Mick Fleetwood's Zoo; Clayton hooked up with Jimmy Buffett for eight years, and Barrère fell deep into drug addiction and recorded two solo albums that he barely remembered making.

In 1986, the owner of The Alley (a former Little Feat rehearsal space) informed Barrère of the venue's Little Feat *homage* – a newly-painted ceiling sporting the *Waiting for Columbus* artwork, and a bathroom wall mural that was a touching portrait of a guitar-slingin' George moseying down a dirt path. The owner suggested a jam session to christen the room, but Barrère was hesitant – an attempted reunion the previous year hadn't gone well, and he wasn't sure anyone would want to relive that.

It just so happened that everyone was in town at the right time, and the informal jam took place. Barrère recalled to Bud Scoppa: 'That's when the magic came back. We'd played old Feat songs. Some we could get through, others we'd get to a certain point and go, 'Oh my God, where does it go from here?' It was funny and fun. Everyone was healthy, more mature and had their wits about them.' Payne agreed: 'What happened that night was pretty darn special, so Paul and I started talking about what we should do about it.'

But just because they'd had one good night didn't mean they were suddenly back together. Clayton was still committed to Buffett, Gradney and Hayward accepted an offer to tour with Warren Zevon, and Payne was about to spend a year on the road with Bob Seger. However, Barrère and Payne realized that the sum of the remaining parts could still make a decent racket, and they proposed a future reunion – schedules permitting – to which the rhythm section tentatively agreed. With the wheels now in motion, Barrère and Payne started piecing a band together: the most obvious addition being Fred Tackett, who just happened to be on tour with Payne.

But there was still a Lowell-George-sized hole to fill. Robert Palmer was suggested first – his Little Feat connection to going back to his 1974 album, *Sneakin' Sally Through the Alley*, which featured a cover of 'Sailin' Shoes' and George on guitar. The following year, the entire band guested on Palmer's *Pressure Drop*, which George produced.

At this point, Palmer had just achieved massive success with 'Addicted To Love' and the Power Station's 'Some Like It Hot.' Though he met with Payne and discussed the Little Feat idea, he ultimately passed, content with his solo career. Bonnie Raitt's name was also thrown around, but a formal offer was never made – besides, she wanted to focus on her solo career too, and was just around the corner from mainstream success.

Then, out of the blue, Craig Fuller called up. When Little Feat broke up in 1979, and George was touring his solo album, Barrère and Payne had formed a new band with Fuller as vocalist, Rick Shlosser on drums, Bob Glaub on bass and Bobby LaKind on percussion, but George's death put an end to the band. In the intervening years, Fuller reformed Pure Prairie League, and wrote 'Hate To Lose Your Lovin'' with Barrère in 1987. So when Fuller called Payne up just to chat, and the keyboardist told him about reforming Little Feat and their difficulty in securing a singer, Fuller naturally suggested he should do it. Payne agreed, and Fuller met up with him and Barrère, sang 'Cold, Cold, Cold,' and they knew they had found the missing puzzle piece.

But when it came to Little Feat's songwriting, times had changed. What used to be the bizarre eccentricity of George's 'cracked mosaics' and Payne's indulgent tendencies, wasn't the kind of thing that would earn them airplay. Besides, Fuller was a more chart-conscious songwriter (his best-known song is Pure Prairie League's earworm 'Amie'), and he was determined to write songs that could be radio hits instead of making artistic statements. Payne agreed, though he wanted to maintain the spirit of the original band, so he suggested that he and Barrère handle the more bluesy left-field stuff, and Fuller sing the more commercial material.

As the songwriting continued into 1988, the momentum was building, though the band still didn't have a manager or record label. Peter Asher (of Peter and Gordon fame) had managed Linda Ronstadt in the 1970s, producing several of her albums and three for James Taylor. Given the George/Ronstadt connection, it wasn't surprising that Asher was familiar with the band and readily accepted when asked to manage them. Though unsure whether Little Feat would have the same draw without Lowell George, Asher was sold on the reformed Feat's demo tape, and played it to Lenny Waronker, who was now the Warner Bros. President. Initially wary of signing them, especially without George, upon hearing the tape, Waronker agreed immediately.

Sessions started in spring 1988 at The Complex in West Los Angeles: the studio owned by familiar face George Massenburg, who co-produced the album with Payne. The band stuck to a regimented schedule, working six days a week for five weeks. Barrère preferred this method, telling Ben Fong-Torres: 'There weren't so many surprises in the studio as on past projects. There was no bullshit in the studio that would've gone on before. There weren't any petty arguments.' The band had a lot to prove, not only to the record label, but to themselves. Barrère told Scoppa: 'We're not only making a record that is going to be stacked up against the Bruce Springsteens and Bob Segers of the world, but it's also going to be stacked up against these last eight records that we did as Little Feat. Quite frankly, if it wasn't going to cut the mustard, we weren't going to do it.' But it did cut the mustard. After a playback of the final mixes, Warner Bros. executives were enthusiastic: a response Barrère found 'cathartic ... like we were healed from that dark period.'

Released on 3 August 1988, *Let It Roll* peaked at 36 in the US: the third Little Feat album to reach that position. Adorned with a surprisingly sedate and nondescript Neon Park cover, the album was a no-nonsense affair. The fans were pleased enough, but reviews were hard to come by. Of the major music magazines, only *Rolling Stone* gave it any column space, though they *were* complimentary: noting that the band sounded 'almost as fresh as it did the first time around.' In a glowing review titled 'Thank Goodness For Pitter-Patter Of Little Feat', the *Orlando Sentinel* observed that 'The songwriting isn't as rich with the imagery of, say, the South or the open highway as classic Feat tunes such as 'Oh Atlanta' or 'Willin'.' But the spirit of this album, created by musicians obviously having a ball playing together again, is a joy to share.'

The next step was to promote the record, and that meant hitting the road, though the band had no intention of making a grand, sweeping return to the stage. Tackett secured a slot at the New Orleans Jazz Festival, where they could slip onto a side stage and work out their repertoire without too much fanfare – that is until noted curmudgeon Van Morrison dropped out and Little Feat were shifted into his slot: performing on the riverboat *Steamboat President*. Payne told Scoppa: 'Suddenly, everybody on the planet knew we were going to play, so, as opposed to us sneaking in under the curtain, the spotlight was on us like nothing we'd ever felt before.'

It helped that they had some friends along for moral support: among them, Clayton's current employer Jimmy Buffett. When Clayton recognized that Little Feat would actually be reuniting, he was hesitant to fully commit out of fear of losing the job security. But his boss insisted, and even offered to take them out on the road as his support act. Clayton told Scoppa: 'We thought that was a great idea. He came onstage when we were opening for him, and told the people to get in their seats, because this band's gonna play. He'd have the house packed for us. He was great. We just played and got it going like he wanted us to. That was the beginning of it all.'

'Hate To Lose Your Lovin'' (Paul Barrère, Craig Fuller)
US A-side (27728), 16 September 1988

Little Feat mean business with this tough but loose boogie rocker – convoluted rhythm, absurd lyrics and female backing vocals; not to mention that scorching bottleneck sound. Fuller and Barrère – who share lead vocals – wrote the song in 1987 as an exploratory collaboration, but Little Feat transformed it into a 'Fat Man In The Bathtub'/'Two Trains' hybrid, and it's like no time has passed at all.

Released as the album's first single, it missed the *Billboard* Hot 100 chart but soared to the top of the Album Rock Tracks chart. (Now known as the Mainstream Rock chart, this offshoot was launched in 1981 to rank the most-played songs on commercial rock stations).

The band performed it on their only *Saturday Night Live* appearance, on 17 December 1988.

'One Clear Moment' (Paul Barrère, Craig Fuller, Bill Payne)
US A-side (27684), October 1988

This is a light, refreshing chaser to the opener, with a nice flashback to 'Romance Dance' (the band searching for a groove in the first few seconds before settling in), but the arrangement is just a little calculated and deliberate. Indeed, it was released as the album's second single but failed to register. Like its predecessor, it did better on the Album Rock Tracks chart, peaking at 10.

'Cajun Girl' (Martin Kibbee, Bill Payne)
US B-side (27728), 16 September 1988

Three songs in, and *Let It Roll* takes a wild left turn, with this appropriately uptempo and zydeco-influenced rocker. Martin Kibbee's first Little Feat songwriting credit since 1974, it's a fun romp, with Fuller flying on button accordion, and – after the abrupt mid-song shift to a samba – Tackett getting a brief mandolin break. Unusually for a Payne song, he doesn't sing on it, leaving it to Barrère to take the lead and Fuller to provide harmony.

'Hangin' On To The Good Times' (Paul Barrère, Craig Fuller, Bill Payne, Fred Tackett)
Inevitably, the band paid tribute to Lowell George and the good ol' days on this lovely upbeat ballad with an intro that borrows heavily from 'Long Distance Love.' The song is neither too maudlin nor sentimental, and the gentle

references to the 'Fat Man In The Bathtub' characters Spotcheck Billy and
Juanita elicit a smile without coming off as heavy-handed.

'Listen To Your Heart' (Craig Fuller, Bill Payne)

This tough and atmospheric rocker is the *Let It Roll* track least characteristic
of Little Feat, and at nearly six minutes long, stands as a challenge to the
fan still on the fence about the reformed Feats. But apart from Barrère's
atypical – if impassioned – guitar solo, the track is a compelling and intriguing
performance, with Fuller's superb vocal perfectly complementing the band's
brooding performance.

'Let It Roll' (Paul Barrère, Martin Kibbee, Bill Payne)

The lyric of the energetic title track uses a sexual encounter as a metaphor
for a road trip, throws in some innuendo – 'Sailin' through her hometown
countryside,' 'When she reach beneath my big ol' steerin' wheel' – and gives it
a contemporary Little Feat sound. It's none of the songwriters' best work, but
it is fun, with the band locking into Hayward's tenacious groove and letting
loose: Payne with a gorgeous Hammond solo, Barrère with some scorching
licks, and Clayton scatting along with the post-chorus melody.

   Though Warner Bros. knew Little Feat didn't stand a chance of scoring a hit
single in 1988, they recognized the landscape had shifted, and with airplay
now having its own *Billboard* chart, they released 'Let It Roll' to DJs as a
promo CD single, it eventually reaching three on the Album Rock Tracks chart.
A traditional vinyl 7' single was released in Europe and Australia, but not in
the US or UK. Instead, the track was promoted through a music video, which
attempted a loose narrative (A buxom bombshell attempts to hitchhike to a
Little Feat concert already in progress, the band miming to the track on a small
dive bar stage), and a performance on *Saturday Night Live*.

'Long Time Till I Get Over You' (Paul Barrère, Craig Fuller)

The mood cools down a bit with this muscular rocker, driven by Hayward's
drumming, with Fuller chastising himself for falling for the same woman:
'And every time I start to feelin' stronger/You call me up with just the right
line.' Barrère's stinging guitar solo and Payne's Hammond organ color the
arrangement, while Fuller, at his full-throated best, is backed up by a superb
sextet of backing singers on the choruses.

   Though not released as a conventional single, 'Long Time' was released as a
one-track promo CD for radio, even charting at 19 in *Billboard*'s Album Rock
Tracks chart.

'Business As Usual' (Paul Barrère, Craig Fuller, Bill Payne)

This overt *message* song – Little Feat's first – takes aim at the increasing
popularity of the 24-hour-news channels and the need for sensational

headlines and stories. Instead of castigating the source of the problem, the songwriters simply observe the torrent of bad news and capitalism disguised as religion, sighing it all off as business-as-usual.

Tucked away at the album's tail end, Hayward propels this tough rocker with a driving, chugging rhythm embellished with expert flourishes. Payne and Barrère also shine – the former adding some lovely piano and keyboard touches, while the latter delivers an absolutely scorching guitar solo. They would go on to write far more effective *message* songs, but this isn't bad for a start.

'Changin' Luck' (Craig Fuller, Bill Payne, Fred Tackett)
US B-side (27684), October 1988

Fuller and Payne team up – with help from Tackett, who likely contributed the opening guitar lick – on this atmospheric epic. Hayward, Clayton, and Gradney lock into the insistent, propulsive rhythm, over which Fuller sings of disillusionment: his own – 'I'd sure like to feel/Dreams I chased so long ago/ Weren't wasted miles on empty roads' – and others' – 'I'd just like to believe/All these desperate cries I hear/Are falling on a sympathetic ear'. Payne, Barrère, and Tackett hold back until nearly three minutes in, when the clouds part and an air of optimism lifts the mood: Payne takes the lead as the voice of sympathy, supported by layers of guitars, keyboards, and backing vocalists.

A rather minor edit – from 6:18 down to 5:51 – was released as the B-side of 'One Clear Moment.'

'Voices On The Wind' (Paul Barrère, Craig Fuller, Bill Payne, Fred Tackett)
The album closes with Fuller singing this classy epic that evokes walking along the ocean at sunset. But a deeper look at the lyric reveals the darker, more poignant reality of a refugee – whether emotional or political – 'Searching for safe passage as you knock on every door,' haunted by 'the howling of the mongrel dogs of war.' Singer Linda Ronstadt elevates this gentle power ballad, swooping in as the voice of reassurance, comforting the scared asylum seeker with, 'There's a light to guide you home.' Fuller and Ronstadt's chorus harmonies are utterly sublime, and the production allows the arrangement to breathe – tiny details like Clayton's percolating congas, Gradney's fretless bass pops, or Barrère's weepy bottleneck, shining just enough over Hayward's gently propelling drums.

Representing the Mambo (1990)

Personnel:

Paul Barrère: guitar, vocals; dobro on 'Those Feat'll Steer Ya Wrong Sometimes'; lead vocal on 'Texas Twister,' 'Woman In Love,' 'Rad Gumbo,' 'That's Her, She's Mine' and 'The Ingenue'

Sam Clayton: percussion, vocals; lead and scat vocals on 'The Ingenue'

Craig Fuller: vocals; rhythm guitar on 'Feelin's All Gone'

Kenny Gradney: bass

Richie Hayward: drums, vocals

Bill Payne: piano, keyboards, vocals; synth horns on 'Texas Twister' and 'Woman In Love'; horn arrangement on 'The Ingenue'; lead vocal and dialogue coach on 'Representing The Mambo'; lead vocal on 'Silver Screen'

Fred Tackett: guitar, trumpet

Additional personnel:

Renée Armand: backing vocals on 'Those Feat'll Steer Ya Wrong Sometimes'

Peter Asher and Neon Park: dialogue on 'Representing The Mambo'

Michael Brecker: saxophone on 'The Ingenue'

Sharon Celani: backing vocals and dialogue on 'Representing The Mambo'

Marilyn Martin: backing vocals on 'Representing The Mambo' and 'Silver Screen'; dialogue on 'Representing The Mambo'

Shaun Murphy: backing vocals on 'That's Her, She's Mine'

Recorded at the Skywalker Ranch, Marin County; Ocean Way, Hollywood; The Hit Factory, New York.

Producers: George Massenburg, Bill Payne

Release date: US: 10 April 1990

Peak position: US: 45

Running time: 50:57

Confident that *Let It Roll* had re-established Little Feat with a slicker, more polished sound, Payne wanted the follow-up to push the envelope further. Two new songs – 'Texas Twister' and 'Rad Gumbo' – were road-tested late on the band's 1989 tour, while Payne refined a song of his own: the title track, that 'had been in my repertoire for years.' With George Massenburg being a friend of filmmaker George Lucas, Little Feat abandoned the familiarity of Los Angeles for Lucas' Skywalker Ranch. Payne told Bud Scoppa: 'I think this came down because Ronstadt was dating Lucas, or had been.' The band worked on new material from autumn 1989 into early-1990, stretching beyond their comfort zone. In the same interview, a rueful Payne said: 'It was my decision, and I kicked myself in the ass about it later. It wasn't exactly a disaster, but not the best move in terms of keeping our career going.'

The problem was that Warner Bros. wanted another *Let It Roll*. Presented with the final *Representing the Mambo* mixes, an exasperated Lenny Waronker asked Payne, 'Man, don't you guys have anything that's more ... rock 'n' roll?' Why Waronker should expect anything straightforward from Little Feat, is anyone's guess – what had made the band so unique and popular in the first place were the 'cracked mosaics' of Lowell George's songwriting, or Payne and Barrère's later left-field experiments. *Let It Roll* had smoothed over those idiosyncrasies enough, but only temporarily.

As the record's producer and prime mover, Payne had to explain himself to Warner Bros., citing 'Texas Twister' and 'That's Her, She's Mine' as having potential radio appeal, but when they strongly suggested the album title be changed, he dug his heels in. In 2014 he told rhino.com:

If we'd called that record *Texas Twister*, I don't know what would've happened, but I'd bet we would've probably been okay in terms of a good follow-up to *Let It Roll*. Neon even painted another cover for it. He says, 'Yeah, but do you think that would've helped?' I said, 'Yeah, I do. Perception is everything.' Perceptions and expectations. So I'm glad we put it out as *Representing the Mambo*. But I knew enough to think, 'Gee, what if we'd done something different?' and Neon indulged me on that, which I thought was quite cool.

Of course, Little Feat is a band, not Payne's band, and the songwriting credits were generously distributed (The only solo credit is Fuller's 'Feelin's All Gone.' All others were written in collaboration by a minimum of at least three writers.), so any album concerns would've been aired and addressed before release. Barrère told Indiana concert critic Marc Allan in 1992:

Let It Roll was probably the safest mainstream kind of rock and roll record of them all. *Representing the Mambo* … seemed to go right over a lot of people's head. They tended to forget the Little Feat that was weird. It was like all they wanted to hear from Little Feat was the 'Let It Roll's and the 'Hate To Lose Your Lovin''s – you know, the 'Dixie Chicken' clones or whatever. They forgot all about 'Day At The Dog Races' and the stranger side of Little Feat, and I thought *Representing the Mambo* was just perfect.

A lot of the blame for the record's failure has been laid at Payne's feet, but it really isn't a bad record at all – the band sounds more loose and relaxed than on *Let It Roll*, by now reacquainted and feeding off each other's enthusiasm. Yes, it would've been difficult hearing some of Payne's morc lofty ambitions sharing the airwaves with 'Nothing Compares 2 U', 'Vogue' or 'It Must Have Been Love' (the top singles circa the album release), but Little Feat never was and never were going to be the kind of band to sell boatloads of albums or singles.

Warner Bros. obviously had different ideas, and with a defiant Payne refusing to budge, they limited their support behind the album:

That was the beginning of the end of us at Warner Bros. We finally got out on a technicality. I felt the worst about that in terms of Lenny Waronker, who was a true champion of the band. In a sense, I felt we stabbed him in the back by leaving the label the way we did. He asked us to stay. But there were people there who were not on our side, and I just felt like we were like a canary in a cage.

'Texas Twister' (Bill Payne, Fred Tackett, Paul Barrère, Martin Kibbee)

The most mainstream song of the bunch is an effective opener – from its tricky intro guitar figure to the propulsive rhythm, effective synth horn stabs punctuating. While the album had no singles, 'Texas Twister' was picked up by radio stations that were sympathetic to a more-established act like Little Feat, though any chance of repeating the success of 'Hate To Lose Your Lovin'' or 'Let It Roll' was dashed by Warner's indifference. But there was enough interest for a music video, which found the band again in a dingy, claustrophobic dive bar, while a waitress tries to escape from her antagonistic bartender boss: *Breaking Bad*'s Larry Hankin.

'Daily Grind' (Bill Payne, Craig Fuller, Paul Barrère)

This slinky shuffle rocker is a solid offering, taking umbrage at the monotony of everyday life. Barrère turns in a scorching guitar solo and Fuller's soulful vocals are a highlight.

'Representing The Mambo' (Bill Payne, Fred Tackett, Neon Park, Paul Barrère)

The 'Day At The Dog Races' of the album, this gets a lot of stick for its left-field arrangement and bizarre lyrics. But it's no wilder than the flights of fancy the band indulged in as far back 'Brides Of Jesus' or 'Crazy Captain Gunboat Willie.' The song was one of Payne's older compositions, having been 'in my repertoire for years.' He told Bud Scoppa: 'I wrote it about South America. I had been talking with Neon Park, and he had some poetry he was writing about high-heeled stilettos. I brought him in as a writer on that tune.' (Not quite: the stiletto imagery was used on the next album's 'Down In Flames.' Payne later clarified in a rhino.com interview that the line about the crowd reminding him of Frank, was Park's.)

At nearly six minutes long, it's the album's longest track, but its multiple stylistic shifts, various arrangement and production twists and *audio vérité* of a rambunctious party, helps maintain interest. (Stick around for the concluding punchline to this forbidden tale of *amor*.) It wasn't top-40 material, but not every Little Feat song needed to be a single. It was simply a fun excursion into territories previously unexplored.

'Woman In Love' (Bill Payne, Fred Tackett, Paul Barrère)

Barrère draws the strongest connection to Little Feat's past with this syncopated rocker that tells the tale of a hardworking woman. But instead of

singing of the seedier streetwalkin' women like he did on 'Walkin' All Night,'
Barrère pays homage to a more classy lady of the night – one who 'works twice
as hard as the boys upstairs,' yet 'She puts in more hours for half the wage/
Ain't no wonder this girl's in a rage.' The track benefits from a cool, laid-back
atmosphere and a catchy chorus.

'Rad Gumbo' (Bill Payne, Kenny Gradney, Martin Kibbee, Neon
Park, Paul Barrère, Sam Clayton)
Little Feat head south to New Orleans with this thick stew of zydeco and Cajun
music, where Barrère essentially sings the recipe for a mighty rad gumbo.
Martin Kibbee and Neon Park contributed lyrics, while Gradney and Clayton
earned their first co-writes since the mid-1970s. Frustratingly, the song fades
out just as it gets going: its all-too-brief three-and-a-half-minute running time
the only disappointment.

'Teenage Warrior' (Bill Payne, Craig Fuller, Fred Tackett, Paul
Barrère)
The album stumbles with this snarling mid-tempo rocker. While the lyrics
don't say much, and Fuller sings them as convincingly as he can, Hayward's
aggressive percussive flourishes and Barrère's fiery guitar work save the
song.

'That's Her, She's Mine' (Bill Payne, Paul Barrère, Sam Clayton)
With its syncopated rhythm, jangly piano straight out of 'Dixie Chicken' and
Shaun Murphy's soulful backing vocals, this excellent song is solid and a
potential radio *hit* (in the loosest definition of the word). But bewildered
Warner Bros. executives just couldn't hear its potential. The silver lining was
that Barrère and Payne invited Murphy back to sing on *Shake Me Up*: effectively
laying the groundwork for her eventual promotion.

'Feelin's All Gone' (Craig Fuller)
The only song on the album to be written solely by Fuller, 'Feelin's All Gone'
recalls the aggressive rhythm of 'Teenage Warrior', but its vaguely-Bob-Seger-
inspired arrangement and performance is pleasant, and a Barrère bottlcneck
solo is always welcome, however brief.

'Those Feat'll Steer Ya Wrong Sometimes' (Bill Payne, Craig
Fuller, Fred Tackett, Paul Barrère, Richie Hayward)
It would be easy to dismiss this as an attempt to pander to the country-pop
masses, but the fact that any kind of crossover wasn't even considered likely
means the band were just having a good time. In that light, it's a gentle
C&W and bluegrass pastiche, with the band turning in a delightfully goofy
performance. Tackett and Barrère add mandolin and dobro flourishes,

respectively. Even Fuller – whose twangy vocal dances that fine line between authenticity and parody – sounds like he's having a blast.

While the title would wind up as prophetic irony for Warner Bros., there was no deeper meaning intended. In 2014, Payne told rhino.com:

> That song was originally called 'Ol' Hank'll Steer You Wrong Sometimes,' as in Hank Williams, Jr., but I couldn't call it that because – and I think rightfully – his handlers said, 'Look, he's in enough trouble. We don't need to have you do that!' … What happened was, I got a traffic ticket in Texas following a James Taylor rehearsal up in Dallas. I went down near Waco to visit my folks, and on the way back, I got a speeding ticket. The officer said, 'Son, you was goin' about 80 miles an hour.' I said, 'Well, gee officer, I was listening to Hank Williams, Jr., and the speed just slipped my mind,' and he goes, 'Son, ol' Hank'll steer you wrong sometimes!'

'The Ingenue' (Bill Payne, Craig Fuller, Fred Tackett, Paul Barrère)

Little Feat shift sharply from a gentle C&W parody to this jazz-fusion workout, with an aggressive convoluted arrangement punctuated by Clayton's scat singing. Throaty saxophone comes from the late Michael Brecker – a fifteen-time Grammy-award-winner who appeared on tracks by Steely Dan, Frank Zappa, Herbie Hancock and many others. For those won over by the straightforward radio-friendly rock of *Let It Roll*, this proved to be a challenge. But for those who appreciate the band's weirder side – executing twists and turns as effortlessly as they had fifteen years prior – 'The Ingenue' is a delight.

'Silver Screen' (Bill Payne, Fred Tackett, Paul Barrère)

The album ends with this atmospheric jazz-tinged rocker, with its poetic lyrics written and sung by Payne (Barrère and Tackett helped out with the music). Exhibiting the kind of sympathetic slice-of-life story Payne increasingly favored, 'Silver Screen' finds a woman utterly obsessed with television – 'a broadcast malady' – eschewing all outside stimuli: 'Her perception of reception is her lone reality.' Payne's approach in these songs is simply to observe, but his clever wordplay ('In her hand she's got control/Remote as that may seem') and resigned vocal delivery have a clear bias – she's wasting her life away, escaping from the hardships of life and a 'city full of wishes she shut out long ago.'

Shake Me Up (1991)

Personnel:
Paul Barrère: guitar, slide guitar, vocals; lead vocal on 'Spider's Blues,' 'Things Happen,' 'Boom Box Car' and 'Clownin''
Sam Clayton: percussion, vocals
Craig Fuller: vocals, guitar
Kenny Gradney: bass
Richie Hayward: drums, vocals
Bill Payne: keyboards, vocals
Fred Tackett: guitar, acoustic guitar, trumpet
Additional personnel:
Valerie Carter: backing vocals on 'Loved And Lied To,' 'Don't Try So Hard' and 'Livin' On Dreams'
Shaun Murphy: backing vocals on 'Spider's Blues,' 'Shake Me Up,' 'Things Happen,' 'Fast & Furious' and 'Clownin''
Bonnie Sheridan: backing vocals on 'Things Happen' and 'Clownin''
The Memphis Horns (Wayne Jackson, trumpet; Andrew Love, sax): brass on 'Things Happen'
Recorded at Conway Recording Studios, Hollywood; Castle Oaks Studios, Calabasas
Producers: Bill Payne, George Massenburg
Release date: US: 24 September 1991
Peak position: US: 126
Running time: 53:29

Sessions for *Shake Me Up* started in spring 1991 at Conway Recording in Hollywood. Twelve basic tracks were recorded over three weeks before the band decamped to Castle Oaks in Calabasas, where eleven songs were overdubbed (a twelfth stored away for future use). The band then returned to Conway to mix the album. All they needed now was a record company.

Morgan Creek Films had earned an impressive windfall in the late-1980s with *Young Guns* and *Major League*, but *Robin Hood: Prince of Thieves* and *The Last of the Mohicans* put them on the map. Bryan Adams' '(Everything I Do) I Do It for You' propelled sales of the *Robin Hood* soundtrack. Seeing how successful Disney had been with Hollywood Records, Morgan Creek executives formed a record label to not only distribute their own soundtracks, but to sign artists and musicians. Swayed by the prospect of support from a company that knew what they were doing and had the cash to back it up, Little Feat signed with Morgan Creek Records, delivering the joyous and rollicking *Shake Me Up*: deemed by Payne to be 'the secret album.'

But it shouldn't have been such a secret: the reformed Feats had hit their stride and delivered an album that was the right balance between *Let It Roll* and *Representing the Mambo*, even though the visceral reaction against Payne's more lofty ambitions on the latter, spooked him to the point that he opted to not sing lead on a single song here: the first and, thankfully, only time this would occur. But the songwriting is strong, mixing elements of past and present, and hopes were high that the album would do well. (Bonnie Bramlett (now Sheridan) returned to a Little Feat record for the first time in almost 20 years, joining other Feats Auxiliary members Valerie Carter and Shaun Murphy.)

'The album went absolutely nowhere,' Barrère seethed to Indiana concert critic Marc Allan in 1992. 'I was like, 'Wait a minute, stop the presses. What's going on here? Something's wrong with this picture.' Little Feat records tend to sell over the long period. I mean, it took twelve years for *Feats Don't Fail Me Now* to go gold, and *Dixie Chicken* even longer. So these things are like, they'll be little gems in somebody's time capsule, somewhere.'

The problem was with Morgan Creek, who was distributed through Polygram. This added another layer of complexity. A frustrated Barrère continued to Allan: 'They're still airing out problems that new labels are wont to have … it's tough sometimes to get all the necessary things happening to sell records. When you think, in the scheme of things, how many brand new labels there are, it's pretty frightening … the business has changed, shall we say.'

Wrapped in a typically-bizarre Neon Park sleeve, *Shake Me Up* struggled into the US charts at 126. There was enough of a budget to shoot a video for 'Things Happen,' but things weren't happening enough for Fuller, who, in summer 1993, informed his bandmates that after three albums and six years, he was leaving Little Feat to focus on his family. Not only that – he felt they had no future at Morgan Creek and that they had to make up for the label's deficiencies by playing live more with less financial security.

Morgan Creek was also struggling to stay afloat. Little Feat jumped ship that summer, with Barrère telling Alan Sculley of the *Daily Press*:

It was kind of the old story of the grass looking greener on the other side of the fence, really. And (they) painted a wonderful picture for us to go for, and I think in the final analysis, the problem was that they were an independent label that was signed up, being distributed by a major. But as far as the distributors were concerned, they were still just an independent label. So they didn't really get the attention they needed as far as their distribution and promotion, and hence it turned out to be one of our worst-selling records ever.

The band was dealt one final blow that year: on 1 September, Neon Park succumbed to Lou Gehrig's disease. Though he designed the *Shake Me Up* sleeve, *Representing the Mambo* was his final submitted sleeve, though several others existed in his archives. After Park's death, Barrère promised in the *Ain't Had Enough Fun* liners that 'as long as there is a Little Feat record, there will be a Neon Park work of art adorning the cover.' For the better part of a decade, they kept that promise.

'Spider's Blues (Might Need It Sometime)' (Bill Payne, Fred Tackett, Paul Barrère)

This loose and lazy boogie-rocker tells the story of the tall and gangly Spider, Lucy – the gal of his dreams – and their hastened (and ultimately abandoned) nuptials. While Barrère weaves Spider's tale, guest vocalist Shaun Murphy provides Lucy's voice: clearly relishing the role's theatrics, even if she does ham it up a bit. A breakdown featuring Tackett's boozy trumpet solo and Payne's rollicking barrelhouse piano, is an obvious nod to 'Dixie Chicken.' Otherwise, the band sound refreshed and rejuvenated, ready to erase the bad memories of *Representing the Mambo* and start afresh.

'Shake Me Up' (Bill Payne, Craig Fuller, Martin Kibbee, Paul Barrère)

The title track is taken at breakneck speed – a disciplined Hayward keeping it going for a full five minutes while his bandmates throw in little touches and flourishes: Payne flies around the piano as Barrère and Tackett trade guitar solos. But the song doesn't say too much, serving more as a dumping ground for disconnected phrases, but with a soulful chorus: Shaun Murphy's backing vocals prominent.

A radio edit was issued as a promo CD, but not commercially.

'Things Happen' (Bill Payne, Fred Tackett, Paul Barrère)

This is a sumptuous radio-friendly foray into Memphis soul, with Barrère passionately singing of overcoming adversity – even throwing in a bittersweet nod to the band's own struggles ('Thought I knew what I wanted/Y'know, be a big success/And to get what I wanted/I just had to do my best') – with support from the powerful combination of Shaun Murphy and Bonnie Sheridan on backing vocals. In a fair and just world, this would've been a hit, but Morgan Creek's attempts were all for nothing. Perhaps they should've released the single in the US, instead of the UK and Europe only. (A special-edition CD sampler – including 'Things Happen,' 'Loved And Lied To,' 'Fast & Furious' and contemporary live versions of 'Oh Atlanta' and 'Rocket In My Pocket' – was released to radio.) A music video was reported to have been filmed in Nashville, but there's no trace of its existence on the internet.

'Mojo Haiku' (Bill Payne, Craig Fuller)

Payne and Fuller team up for this unusual composition, which marries an aggressive rock arrangement to an abstract lyric about the many ways to communicate love: 'She brought some fundamental passions into play/ No doubt about it, I felt the darkness start to slip away', 'I'm talkin' bout the land beyond the pale/The kinda thing that ain't for sale'. Hayward rolls around his drum set, trying to hit every drum and cymbal while keeping the mid-tempo rhythm moving (slipping into a welcome syncopated pattern in the pre-chorus), while Barrère and Tackett funk it up a bit on guitars. 'Mojo

Haiku' is a worthy experiment that scratches the itch for the fan looking for left-field Feat.

'Loved And Lied To' (Bill Payne, Craig Fuller, Paul Barrère, Richie Hayward)
The album slows down with this gentle power-ballad, featuring a lyric that's largely the work of Hayward: his second after 'Tripe Face Boogie.' The song evokes an easy, breezy, mid-1970s California feelin', thanks to Payne's electric piano and Barrère's flanged guitar solo. Fuller even gets close to replicating Lowell George's vibe. But Valerie Carter's backing vocals are what solidify the track's status – not only as an album highlight, but as a song that could easily rub shoulders with Little Feat's early material and not be out of place.

'Don't Try So Hard' (Craig Fuller)
This is a pleasant mid-tempo pop-rocker that, despite treading well-worn ground – Fuller's unlucky in love and won't repeat the same mistakes – is one of his better songs. Barrère gets a bottleneck solo, and Payne dusts off the Hammond for some extra texture: all adding up to a solid offering.

'Boom Box Car' (Paul Barrère)
Ever wanted to hear Barrère yell at the youth to turn their rap music down, and that back in his day, the kids would take their dates to Blueberry Hill and get up to no good in the back of their Chevys? No? Me neither. *Shake Me Up* would've been an even 49 minutes without this song.

'Fast & Furious' (Bill Payne, Fred Tackett, Paul Barrère, Sam Clayton)
This up-tempo rocker roars along at breakneck speed, as Fuller croons mightily about his love: the loose 'n' easy Sally. There's not much to sink your teeth into here, but the band are clearly having a ball, and Shaun Murphy's prominent backing vocals were a good call.

'Livin' On Dreams' (Bill Payne, Craig Fuller, Fred Tackett, Paul Barrère)
This atmospheric rocker starts off with some clever wordplay ('Another grey dawn, another day gone') but is otherwise fairly generic, though Fuller is at his full-throated best. The arrangement is graced with little touches – some dobro here, some Hammond organ there – that add to the mood, but it's Valerie Carter's harmony vocal that really make the song.

'Clownin'' (Fred Tackett, Paul Barrère)
Tackett and Barrère deliver a late-album highlight with this funky, good time rocker: a vibe right out of 1973. Fed up with his two-timing woman, Barrère

takes her to task, calling out her desperate bids for attention and romantic mind games: 'So won't you please stop your teasin'/ Y'know you got no reason/ To be clownin' with my heart.'

'Down In Flames' (Bill Payne, Craig Fuller, Martin Kibbee, Neon Park, Paul Barrère)

Shake Me Up concludes with this atmospheric epic that benefits from Kibbee and Park's lyrical input. By this point, Park was battling the degenerative disease ALS, and he had to give up his first love painting, for poetry, which wasn't as physically taxing. Payne caught wind of Park's poetry and used some in both 'Representing The Mambo' and 'Down in Flames.' In the case of the latter, it was the lines 'Here with my memento and her air of mystery/One high-heeled stiletto, what did she ever mean to me?'

'Down In Flames' fails to reach the same heights as previous album closers 'Voices On The Wind' or 'Silver Screen,' but the performance is top-notch, with Fuller especially in fine voice. Indeed, it served as his swan song – frustrated with the lack of success and the band's fall from grace (they left Morgan Creek Records after this one album), Fuller gave notice in summer 1993. While some of his songwriting choices or approaches sat at odds with the familiar Little Feat sound, Fuller had given the band the shot in the arm they needed, and there's no denying that without his enthusiasm, energy and drive, the second half of their career wouldn't have been half as successful.

Related Track
'Quicksand And Lies' (Bill Payne, Craig Fuller)

The twelfth song Barrère referenced in the album liner notes is a driving, cinematic power ballad with a solid Fuller vocal (with backing vocal by Valerie Carter). It played over the end credits of Morgan Creek's *White Sands*: a 1992 box-office disappointment starring Willem Dafoe, Mary Elizabeth Mastrantonio and Mickey Rourke. It's not a Little Feat classic by a long shot, but it is distinctive in its obscurity: consigned to the soundtrack and a promotional two-track CD single (consisting of a four-minute radio edit and the full version). The track has yet to appear on any archival or retrospective compilation, and has apparently been completely forgotten (It's not mentioned anywhere on the band's website).

Ain't Had Enough Fun (1995)

Personnel:
Paul Barrère: guitar, dobro, vocals; lead vocal on 'Cajun Rage,' 'Shakeytown' and 'Ain't Had Enough Fun'; co-lead vocal on 'Romance Without Finance' and 'Big Bang Theory'
Sam Clayton: percussion, vocals; co-lead vocal on 'Romance Without Finance'
Kenny Gradney: bass
Richie Hayward: drums, vocals
Shaun Murphy: vocals, percussion
Bill Payne: keyboards, vocals; horn arrangement on 'Romance Without Finance'; lead vocal on 'Blue Jean Blues'; co-lead vocal on 'Borderline Blues'
Fred Tackett: guitar, mandolin
Additional personnel:
Van Dyke Parks: accordion on 'Ain't Had Enough Fun'
Piero Mariani: electronic percussion on 'Drivin' Blind,' 'Blue Jean Blues,' 'Borderline Blues,' 'Heaven's Where You Find It,' 'Cajun Rage' and 'All That You Can Stand'
The Texicali Horns (Joe Sublett, tenor saxophone; Darrell Leonard, trumpet; David Woodford, tenor and baritone saxophone) on 'That's A Pretty Good Love,' 'Cadillac Hotel,' 'Rock And Roll Everynight' and 'Blue Jean Blues'
Darrell Leonard: horn arrangement on 'Romance Without Finance'
Recorded at Ocean Way, Hollywood; Groove Masters, Santa Monica
Producers: Bill Payne, Bill Wray
Co-producer and engineer: Ed Cherney
Release date: US: 25 April 1995
Peak position: US: 154
Running time: 69:56

The Morgan Creek fiasco had thrown a wrench in the band's works. In July 1993, Barrère told the *Daily Press*' Alan Sculley:

We were planning on going out and recording another live record, since it's been fifteen years since our last live record ... and then all this came down, so there's been a change in direction, and now we're focusing in on writing new songs and stuff because we know if we get a new deal, they're not going to want to have a live record first thing off the bat.

Craig Fuller's departure in September further complicated things, but only temporarily – Payne and Barrère had been impressed with Shaun Murphy's singing – which became increasingly prominent over the course of the three albums – and she was invited to record some demos at Barrère's house. After running through 'Romance Without Finance,' they simply asked her, 'How would you feel if you found yourself in the middle of the United States on a bus with six guys?' Murphy joined the band officially on 27 September 1993, with her first show on New Year's Eve.

Barrère and Payne were pleased with the addition of Murphy – the former enthusiastically telling Fong-Torres, 'It's an interesting new shade.' Hayward too welcomed the change, telling *Modern Drummer* in October 1995: 'It definitely gave the band a tune-up. It's a whole new direction and approach. I think Shaun's really exciting. She's more R&B, blues and rock-rooted than Craig was. Shaun has this knife-edge to her performances that's really exciting.'

But not everyone was on board – Gradney and Clayton both viewed Little Feat as a guy's club, though Clayton eventually warmed up to Murphy, telling Fong-Torres: 'She's by far the superior vocalist. I'm not sayin' she's better than Lowell, but she's by far the superior vocalist.' Gradney did too, but still couldn't reconcile having 'a chick in the band.' Payne was perplexed by any reservations, saying, 'It was years later that I realized that some band members were not enamored of her being there. I thought, 'Why'd they have to wait fifteen years to say anything?'

What mattered was that fans welcomed Shaun Murphy. She recalled to Fong-Torres an initial mild shock, but that she made it clear she wasn't replacing anybody: '...that I just had my little niche in the band and brought a lot of energy – I turned a lot of minds around. But it was a process, definitely.'

In search of a new label, the band eventually settled on Zoo Records: another start-up with prominent backing (Lou Maglia: former president of Island Records) and a huge distributor (BMG: parent company of RCA). They even had familiar face Bud Scoppa working A&R, so at least they felt somewhat at home. But the label's early success wasn't sustainable, and signing Little Feat was a last effort to regain credibility and recover losses.

After Little Feat's US tour supporting B.B. King, the new album (consisting of twelve originals and one cover) was recorded at Ocean Way in Hollywood, with overdubs taking place at Jackson Browne's Groove Masters in Santa Monica. The band and George Massenburg had parted company amicably.

Payne had found a sympathetic ear in Shreveport-born singer-songwriter Bill Wray: who'd done as Lowell George might've done, and moved his focus to production. Payne and Wray also co-wrote (together or with other Feats members) seven songs, though – according to Fred Tackett – Wray had done his homework on the band. Tackett told the *Tampa Bay Times* in 2005:

He was good at adding those little old-style touches to our songs. He'd say something like, 'Play one of those stumbling-type drum licks like you did at this show way back when,' or 'Play this the way you did it on this particular album.' Sometimes in your quest to improve, you get so caught up in what's happening now, that you forget what was cool about what you did before. Making this album reminded us of who we were.

Released in April 1995, *Ain't Had Enough Fun* (true to their word, the band used a Neon Park painting for the cover) was met with indifference. It stumbled to 154 in *Billboard*, and earned a scathing review from Chuck Eddy in *Entertainment Weekly*: 'More songful than any young retro jam-band on the charts, these old field hands still cook up a loose-limbed Cajun-boogie brew. Too bad the warm, open-ended tunes are almost all more than five minutes long. Equally unfortunate is new female vocalist Shaun Murphy, whose stodgy growls belong in a beer commercial.'

John Moran in the *Hartford Courant* was a little more charitable:

Murphy's bold and smoky voice, takes right over on 'Drivin' Blind': a mixture of African rhythms and Cajun harmonies. And it remains prominent right through the final cut 'That's A Pretty Good Love': a hot boogie-woogie blues ... *Ain't Had Enough Fun* doesn't seem to have any of the infectious FM radio cuts that have gotten the Feat so much airplay since the band regrouped. It's possible, perhaps even likely, that the band can infuse tremendous energy into these songs in concert ... But the translation of the Little Feat live performance to recorded disc, remains an elusive goal.

Once again, record label issues plagued the promotion of a decent album. Murphy gave the band a new energy, and hopes were high that Zoo would be able to achieve a hit. But the music industry had again shifted, as had radio – 'Shakeytown' snuck out as a promo single in 1995, but there just wasn't any space on the dial for a band like Little Feat. So they toured, and then toured some more, with over 150 shows performed in 1995 alone. The band's long-delayed second live album *Live From Neon Park* was released on 18 June 1996 (Barrère quipped in the liner notes: 'I am reasonably confident that a day in Neon Park could never be confused with a day in the Grand Canyon. Neon Park is much deeper ... and has a better view.'), but that was it for Feats on Zoo. Just two months after the live album's release, BMG sold the label to Volcano Entertainment, initially as a partnership. But by the end of the following year, Zoo ceased to exist and Volcano was now the home for all former Zoo artists. Except for Little Feat. They had another trick up their sleeves, and it involved this new thing called the information superhighway.

'Drivin' Blind' (Bill Payne, Bill Wray)
This Cajun-inspired boogie rocker serves as the perfect introduction for Murphy, who is at her full-throated best as she sings of the uncertainty of youth and what lies ahead. The band sound rejuvenated and energetic – undoubtedly the result of their new record label and the enthusiasm of Murphy and co-producer Bill Wray. That October, Hayward singled out the song for *Modern Drummer* as 'really fun and has a great drum part. I tried to find a basic pattern for it that was eight bars long and didn't repeat itself – something that I could basically repeat throughout the song and embellish on in subtle ways.'

Ending the track is a 35-second instrumental jam with Tackett on mandolin, Payne on synthesized accordion and Hayward on drums. This untitled piece would be revisited and expanded upon in 1998's 'Calling The Children Home.'

'Blue Jean Blues' (Paul Barrère, Bill Payne, Bill Wray, Fred Tackett)

Payne takes the lead on this laid-back groove piece – an ode to a 'perfect girl living in a perfect world,' with Murphy and Barrère on backing vocals. The three-piece Texicali Horns make their debut on a Little Feat album, and would show up periodically on subsequent albums. Their performance here is subtle and understated, complementing Hayward's muscular drumming and Barrère's bottleneck.

'Cadillac Hotel' (Bill Payne, Bill Wray)

In *Modern Drummer*, Hayward singled out 'Cadillac Hotel' as 'what Little Feat is all about. It was that 'Rock And Roll Doctor,' 'Dixie Chicken' kind of feel. When Billy brought it into rehearsal, it was like putting on a comfortable old pair of shoes that still had a shine on them. It's not derivative enough of our old stuff to be the same old baked potato – at least we hope not anyway.'

It's hard to disagree. This cool, slinky, bluesy shuffle not only sounds closest to the band's past, but also name-checks 'Eldorado Slim': a nice bit of self-reference that those who'd been with the band from the beginning, would get. The band is firing on all cylinders here, but Murphy is the star of the show, turning in a powerful vocal (which Barrère's bottleneck follows) as she sings what can only be a defiant battle cry: 'I've climbed so high/And I've sure fell/ Ten thousand feet to zero.'

'Romance Without Finance' (Bill Payne, Martin Kibbee, Sam Clayton)

Set to a stumbling drum pattern and a rolling barrelhouse piano, this song finds an unlucky-in-love Murphy bemoaning the allure of financial security at the cost of true love, even if, in the end, she chooses the latter. Written by Payne, Kibbee and Clayton (who also provides prominent backing vocals), the song is as fun to listen to as it sounds like it was to record.

'Big Bang Theory' (Bill Payne, Bill Wray, Fred Tackett, Paul Barrère, Shaun Murphy)

The album shifts into high gear with this fun rocker, even if the subject matter is rather hackneyed. Murphy, the nagging wife and Barrère the lazy husband, race through a litany of misdeeds, only to conclude that opposites attract and that's just how love is. But it doesn't matter what they're singing; the band is having a blast, and their enthusiasm is infectious, with Barrère going to town on bottleneck, Tackett flying along right beside him. Payne extemporizes on Hammond, as Hayward, Clayton and Gradney hold down the chugging rhythm.

'Cajun Rage' (Bill Wray, Martin Kibbee, Paul Barrère)

Little Feat make a welcome return to New Orleans on this boisterous boogie rocker, with Barrère gleefully leering through each verse as he provides an update of sorts to 'Romance Dance.' (The title is a bedroom act, as is the 'couchez fandango' and 'the nude lambada.') The gusto for not only the subject matter but the arrangement, is palpable: as elsewhere on the album, the band is clearly enjoying themselves, especially when they answer Barrère's lines in the chorus. The song became an immediate live favorite – a regular on their 1995 dates, subsequent tours featured it only occasionally.

'Heaven's Where You Find It' (Bill Payne, Fred Tackett, Paul Barrère, Shaun Murphy)

Murphy is again fed up – this time because the man of her liking complains too much and isn't reciprocating her affection. Set to a lumbering rhythm, this impassioned slow burn is a superb performance. Hayward shines on drums, a hardworking Barrère flies away on bottleneck, but it's Murphy that again steals the show with her powerful vocal. Except for a few cornpone expressions ('We got somethin' goin'/Sweeter than a buckwheat cake,' 'You always think the grass is greener/I got more than you need, right here at home'), 'Heaven's Where You Find It' is a fine track and an undisputed album highlight.

'Borderline Blues' (Bill Payne, Bill Wray, Fred Tackett, Paul Barrère, Shaun Murphy)

Neon Park's death from Lou Gehrig's disease on 1 September 1993 was a devastating blow to Little Feat's personality. Discounting their debut album, Park's artwork was an inarguable piece of the Little Feat puzzle. But now, they had one less connection to their past. Lowell George was the band's heart, but Park had been their visual focal point.

Profoundly affected by Park's death, Payne poured his grief into lyrics, writing most of what became 'Borderline Blues': the album's undoubted highlight. Payne and Murphy harmonize beautifully, each taking the lead for a line or two, while the languid arrangement stretches out over seven minutes. Barrère gets a tasteful solo in, while Hayward jumps between drum patterns that use either overly-florid cymbals or none whatsoever. He told *Modern Drummer*: 'I simplified what Manu Katché does with Peter (Gabriel), but I like the way he can establish a really exciting feel with just a tom/snare kind of thing. I can't play like Manu, so I did my own version.'

This beautiful track is poignant without being overly sentimental, and is best experienced in its full glory – avoid the edited version on the *Hotcakes and Outtakes* box set, which credits the song as the single version, despite it never being released as one.

'All That You Can Stand' (Bill Payne, Bill Wray, Paul Barrère)

Little Feat here conjure up a thick, spooky witchcraft stew, the band trying their best to channel the spirit of Dr. John. They mostly succeed – Tackett's mandolin and Hayward's flashy cymbal work give the song an otherworldly feel, while Payne's Hammond solo is brief but effective.

'Rock And Roll Everynight' (Bill Payne, Bill Wray, Fred Tackett, Paul Barrère, Shaun Murphy)
On this jubilant track, Murphy gives it her all as she extols the benefits of being a traveling musician, while Barrère answers her every line with scorching bottleneck guitar, and Payne delivers a piano solo straight out of 'Oh Atlanta.'

'Shakeytown' (Martin Kibbee, Paul Barrère)
This searing, soaring boogie rocker – about an aspiring actress making her way to the top ('And now she's off in a corner/With a Hollywood wheel/Lookin' to hook a development deal for fifty grand, honey/And all she can steal') – absolutely cooks, with the band sounding as rough and raw as they did in concert. Surprisingly, Zoo Records issued this as a promo CD single, but it garnered little airplay.

'Ain't Had Enough Fun' (Bill Payne, Chick Strand, Fred Tackett, Paul Barrère, Shaun Murphy)
The short and sweet title track features Van Dyke Parks on accordion, while Barrère warbles away about livin' the good life. There's also a lyric contribution from Neon Park's widow Chick Strand. This has all the warmth and geniality of a campfire sing-along – its atmosphere natural, airy and light, with the lively gospel chorus accentuated by mandolin, dobro and tambourine.

'That's A Pretty Good Love' (Fred Mendelssohn, Bryant Lucas)
The first cover on a Feats album since 'Don't Bogart That Joint,' 'That's A Pretty Good Love' was made famous by Big Maybelle in May 1956, though blues pianist and singer Charles Brown covered it on his 1990 album *All My Life*. Presumably chosen by Murphy (she covered it on her first post-Feats solo album *Livin' the Blues*), this solid blues rocker is a Murphy/Clayton duet, with fiery guitar work from Tackett and Barrère, and rollicking piano from Payne.

Under the Radar (1998)

Personnel:
Paul Barrère: guitar, dobro, dulcimer, harmonica, vocals; lead vocal on 'Home Ground,' 'Loco Motives,' 'Ferocious Morning,' 'I Got Happiness' and 'Calling The Children Home'
Sam Clayton: percussion, vocals
Kenny Gradney: bass, vocals
Richie Hayward: drums, little tyke playhouse, vocals
Shaun Murphy: vocals, tamborine
Bill Payne: keyboards, vocals; horn arrangement on 'Eden's Wall' and 'Calling The Children Home'; lead vocal on 'Eden's Wall' and 'Under the Radar'
Fred Tackett: guitar, dobro, trumpet, vocals
Additional personnel:
Lenny Castro: percussion on 'Home Ground' and 'Eden's Wall'
Piero Mariani: percussion on 'Falling Through The Worlds,' 'The Blues Don't Tell It All' and 'Calling The Children Home'
The Texicali Horns (Joe Sublett: saxophone; Darrell Leonard: trumpet, trombonium) on 'Home Ground,' 'Eden's Wall' and 'Calling The Children Home'; horn arrangement on 'Home Ground'
Darrell Leonard: horn transcription on 'Eden's Wall' and 'Calling The Children Home'
Recorded at Yohoyville Studios East, Woodland Hills, and Yohoyville Studios West, Calabasas; Westlake Studios, Hollywood: 'Home Ground,' 'Eden's Wall' and 'Vale Of Tears'
Producers: Bill Payne, Paul Barrère
Production and engineering assistance: Bill Wray, Ed Cherney: 'Home Ground,' 'Eden's Wall' and 'Vale Of Tears'
Release date: US: 16 June 1998
Peak position: US: -
Running time: 70:32

By the end of 1996, Little Feat were at a crossroads. Radio had forgotten them, the charts ignored them, and they couldn't even hold down a steady a record contract. The only solution was to play live. They spent most of 1997 on the road. Normally a source of enjoyment, it now soured with it being their only source of income. The year was especially difficult for Payne, who for most of it had an undiagnosed illness which he suspected was an allergic reaction to an antibiotic, and his ex-wife Fran Tate passed away after a battle with cancer.

But there was a light at the end of the darkness. The band signed with CMC International – then home to legacy acts such as Yes, Thin Lizzy and Lynyrd Skynyrd – who'd adapted a new promotional method. ('New tunes, new record label, new hopes for a brighter future,' *The Washington Post* announced, before snarking, 'How many times have we heard that about Little Feat?')

Payne told Bud Scoppa: 'For months I've been asking management how to put together a grassroots organization, and all I hear is 'Oh, they'll get back to us.' So I'm reading Hunter S. Thompson's *Fear and Loathing: On the Campaign Trail '72*, and I go 'Bingo! This is how you do it.'' Inspired by Thompson's coverage of the 1972 US presidential election and George McGovern's grassroots campaign to boost his candidacy, Payne realized that what was missing was communication with the fans: 'So, during this tour, we started asking, 'Hey, are you guys on the internet? You know, we have a website.' They'd say, 'You're kidding.' Two years later, we have thousands of people on board.'

The word-of-mouth approach had to work. Little Feat's days as a chart presence – no matter about their meager showings – were gone, and the only airplay they now got was for their mid-1970s material, so performing live and connecting with the fans was the only logical solution. Payne told Scoppa: 'We're just selfish about the fact that we want to play, that's what all this boils down to. If people are going to take the opportunity away from you, then you fight hard to maintain that opportunity. We relish that. We're in for the fight.'

With a renewed sense of purpose and a record label that was on their side, the band started sessions for the new album after a quick six-week US tour in January and February 1998. Three songs were cut at Westlake Studios in Hollywood, with production assistance from Bill Wray, and the other nine were recorded at Payne and Barrère's home studios: rechristened Yohoyville East (Barrère's home) and Yohoyville West (Payne's home).

The idea to record at home came from CMC International President Tom Lipsky. Barrère wrote in the liner notes: 'He not only approved of the idea of recording at home but encouraged it.' This resulted in a comfortable, organic recording; not that any of the reformed Feats' previous recordings sounded stifled, but their slick sound was largely rectified here, and would continue to be tweaked over successive releases.

Under the Radar ('Kinda how it's been for Little Feat these past 29 years,' Barrère explained in the liner notes; 'Flyin' fast and low') was released on 16 June 1998 and sank without a trace – their first studio album since *Dixie Chicken* not to make a chart showing. The cover was another irreverent Neon Parks painting, this time parodying Michelangelo's The Creation of Adam. (Keen-eyed Feats fans may notice a connection between the toy plane, the man's hand and Lowell George's bottleneck technique.)

If the band was worried, they didn't show it. Tackett told Scoppa in 2000: 'I don't know what's going to happen. It's a tough scene right now. You can't really get any airplay, so you have to use other means of going about it.' Payne agreed, telling Michael B. Smith on swampland.com in 2000:

The internet is a part of the wave of the future. There are a lot of people out there who are tapping into all of that. We have a grassroots organization, and we are switching over to an all-email situation. A lot of bands are doing that because snail mail is so costly. It's just the power of communication. It's so much quicker. The immediacy of it is what you're after, and people are tapping into it on every level of society.

'Home Ground' (Paul Barrère)

This slinky, snarling ode to fidelity ('Don't need no stage door Jenny/No bad luck Penny/Lookin' for a one-night Romeo') with its brass stabs and scorching guitar solo, is one of Barrère's finest compositions in years. Its concise four-minute running time suggests the band thought it might make a suitable radio hit. Indeed, CMC International issued a promo single to radio, though the song was largely ignored.

'Eden's Wall' (Bill Payne, Paul Barrère, Shaun Murphy)

Opening with an ethereal drone and a prog-like guitar figure, 'Eden's Wall' quickly shifts to a soft Cajun rhythm, with Payne taking the lead, singing of a guardian angel 'keepin' me on track.' He later singled out 'Eden's Wall' as particularly noteworthy, telling Scoppa it's 'about not taking anything less than what you're worth; you draw the line in the sand. I asked my son, who's fifteen years old, 'Evan, am I goin' in or out of Eden?' He says, 'You're going out of Eden.' I ask him why. He goes, 'It's more compelling that way.' I said, 'That's a good word, and you're damn right.''

'A Distant Thunder' (Bill Payne, Paul Barrère, Shaun Murphy)

This superb song is a triumph, and especially a showcase for Murphy's considerable vocal talents, as she pays homage to 'those who've come and gone before me.' Chiming mandolins, groaning bottleneck guitars and clattering drums contribute to this masterfully atmospheric track, though it doesn't quite ever reach the emotional heights it seems to be shooting for. The song was released as a single in Europe, and a radio edit was issued as a promotional single in America.

'Hoy Hoy' (Bill Payne, Paul Barrère, Shaun Murphy, Fred Tackett)

Another track just breaking the four-minute barrier, the often-used expression from Little Feat lore finally gets a song. It's just a shame it doesn't really go anywhere. Murphy's singing is superb (backed up in places by *basso profundo* Clayton), Barrère flies on slide guitar, and the ethereal mandolin-driven interstitial mid-section is pleasant.

'Under The Radar' (Bill Payne, Paul Barrère, Shaun Murphy)

It wouldn't be too much of a stretch to presume this song was written for Payne's ex-wife Fran Tate (who passed from cancer the year before), based on the lyrics of this dreamy, summery ballad; Payne sweetly singing of simpler times and stolen kisses. The track's seven minutes stretch out over a gently propulsive rhythm, with soft keyboard touches and a delicate guitar solo. In the final two minutes, Barrère takes flight on slide guitar before Payne takes over on organ.

'Vale Of Tears' (Fred Tackett, Shaun Murphy, Bill Payne)

While a 'vale' is defined as a valley, the phrase 'vale of tears' is a pessimistic definition of a world of pain and suffering; Christianity taking it a step further, regarding it as a place to leave behind when exiting this mortal coil. The song was written in response to the death of Murphy's brother David, and is a dark minor-key acoustic ballad that builds in intensity over six-plus minutes. Murphy's voice is restrained yet impassioned, boosted by Barrère's groaning bottleneck and Payne's shimmering Hammond. A short, economical guitar solo keeps this slow-burning track interesting.

'Loco Motives' (Paul Barrère, Fred Tackett)

Hayward bastardizes the Bo Diddley rhythm before leading the band into this stuttering rocker, which finds Barrère bemoaning the tedium of touring, while dreaming of jumping a train home to get back to his gal. If anything, the *double entendre* of locomotive transportation and locomotives as 'crazy intentions' is worthy of a smile. But the song is actually quite solid, with Payne delivering a manic piano solo as Barrère wails away on bottleneck, approximating the sound of a train tearing out of town.

'Ferocious Morning' (Fred Tackett, Paul Barrère)

Borrowing the melody and rhythm from 'On Your Way Down,' 'Ferocious Morning' is a lush's lighthearted lament, with Barrère playing the hungover narrator: 'I was a real live wire on a very loose wig/Not a good combination in the best of times.' Set to a slinky funk, the track is an experiment in the atypical, with mild concessions to technology – Hayward's treated drums especially – with the added flavor of Tackett's woozy trumpet and Barrère's scorching guitar solo making for an interesting overall result. At the very least, the band accurately capture the spirit of a wild night's aftermath.

'Voiceless Territory' (Bill Payne, Shaun Murphy, Fred Tackett, Paul Barrère)

Lasting barely 50 seconds, this is a mystical-sounding clattering of percussion with swirling keyboards and effects, serving as an introduction to…

'Falling Through The Worlds' (Bill Payne, Shaun Murphy, Paul Barrère, Fred Tackett)

Murphy conjures up more dark spirits on this mystical mood piece. While her vocal is the undisputed highlight, Clayton's percussion and Piero Mariani's bass marimba are nice touches in an otherwise pleasant song.

'The Blues Don't Tell It All' (Bill Payne, Shaun Murphy)

This jolly excursion – with Payne's percolating piano and Hayward's syncopated drum pattern – is a far cry from the blues the title implies. But it's a masterful composition, expertly arranged and performed. The solid-if-gentle groove lends itself well to extemporization, with Payne and Barrère both getting mid-song spotlights. But the band finally starts cooking just as the track begins its long fade-out, with Barrère especially enjoying the freedom to fly around his fretboard.

'I Got Happiness' (Paul Barrère, Shaun Murphy)

This album highlight is set to a boozy, bluesy rhythm, with Barrère doubling on dobro and harmonica; his voice fed through the microphone of the latter, giving a surreal, weathered effect.

'Calling The Children Home' (Bill Payne, Paul Barrère, Shaun Murphy, Fred Tackett)

Payne told Randy Ray on *jambands.com* in 2008:

> There's a phrase from New Orleans. Fred Tackett read it in a biography about Satchmo: Louis Armstrong. He was describing in this book, this call that would go within New Orleans. It was essentially calling the children home, but what they were doing was calling everybody to meet at a gathering place, wherever that might be. This applied to musicians as well as to an audience: 'Let's put on a hoedown. Let's put on a jam.'

So Little Feat did exactly that. Revisiting the brief untitled piece on the end of the previous album's 'Drivin' Blind,' they constructed a sprawling ode to the Crescent City, with Barrère paying homage to the city's party spirit and its musical pioneers – Buddy Bolden: a major figure in the development of jazz; Ernie K. Doe: best-known for his cover of Allen Toussaint's 'Mother-in-Law'; Bobby Marchand: a drag queen and bandleader; Eddie Bo: a jazz, blues and funk pianist who sold more records than anyone from New Orleans (second only to Fats Domino), and – of course – Dr. John the Night Tripper.

The track shifts gear occasionally, with a mid-song breakdown reduced to Payne's barrelhouse piano and Hayward's clattering drums. It kicks into high gear in the final 90 seconds, where the song ends abruptly and Payne leads the band into a raucous boogie shuffle, with Barrère getting in some scorching guitar fills, and Joe Sublett gets a few saxophone wails. Without a doubt, this is one of Little Feat's finest recorded pieces of music.

Related Tracks

'Cat Fever' (Live) (Bill Payne)

Japan bonus track

In consideration of the exorbitant price of compact discs in Japan in the late-1990s, it became common for artists to include a bonus track as an incentive. Little Feat acceded here with this live performance of 'Cat Fever,' though its provenance is unknown. According to featbase.net, the song returned to the setlist in 1997 after a 24-year absence and was performed only twice (on 1 July in Chicago and 12 August in Charlotte, Vermont). But the track is possibly from an otherwise unknown show.

Chinese Work Songs (2000)

Personnel:

Paul Barrère: guitar, dobro, bicycle bells, vocals; lead vocal on 'Rag Mama Rag,' 'Eula,' 'Marginal Creatures' and 'Chinese Work Songs'; co-lead vocal on 'Sample In A Jar'

Sam Clayton: percussion, vocals

Kenny Gradney: bass, vocals

Richie Hayward: drums, vocals; lead vocal on 'Gimme A Stone'

Shaun Murphy: vocals

Bill Payne: keyboards, vocals; co-lead vocal on 'Sample In A Jar' and 'Just Another Sunday'

Fred Tackett: guitar, dobro, vocals

Additional personnel:

The Texicali Horns (Darrell Leonard: trumpet and trombonium; Joe Sublett: saxophone) on 'Rag Mama Rag,' 'Just Another Sunday' and 'Chinese Work Songs'

Béla Fleck: banjo on 'Gimme A Stone'

Lenny Castro and Piero Mariani: percussion

Recorded at Studio Without Walls and Too Many Dogs Studios, Los Angeles

Producers: Paul Barrère, Bill Payne

Release date: US: 20 June 2000

Peak position: US: -

Running time: 61:23

Little Feat's grassroots movement to build their fan base by word of mouth had worked. Without the luxury of a promoter with deep pockets (like other legacy acts had at their disposal), the band simply hit the road, taking copies of the new album with them to sell directly to fans. By the start of 2000, the band's website had several thousand unique visitors and mailing-list subscribers. CMC International also stuck around, leading to some band stability. Sessions for the new album started early in 2000, stretching out over 'years, weeks and days,' according to Barrère in the liner notes. Basic tracks were recorded at Nathaniel Kunkel's Studio Without Walls in Los Angeles, with overdubs cut at Too Many Dog Studios – except for Béla Fleck's contribution to 'Gimme a Stone,' which was done from Nashville by way of CDR.

Payne told *jambands.com* in 2001 that the album 'reflects a transitional phase. In this case, we're at the top of a transition rather than the end of anything. There are three or four tunes from different artists, which makes it remarkably different from most of our records. We did songs by Phish, The Band; a Dylan tune.'

The cover songs may come as a shock, but the band had been ruminating on the idea of a blues covers album, with a handful of songs introduced into the setlists. While that idea didn't pan out, Payne told swampland.com in 2000 that he liked the idea of 'doing some other songs, including the Band tune 'Rag Mama Rag' … I just thought it was a great tune, and I could just hear Paul singing it.'

110

But cracks were beginning to show. Murphy, while a strong vocalist, was less engaged with the older Little Feat songs and often relied on covers. Barrère later complained to Ben Fong-Torres: 'She didn't dive in to find old Feat songs. We would have to suggest certain ones to her. She would do them, but we would always have to bring it up. She never really went for it.' Payne shrugged off any dissension, telling swampland.com: 'Quite honestly, the idea of recording that many covers – because there are four of them on there – we were just looking for good material. We have seven of our own on there too.'

To Murphy's credit, she was still involved in the songwriting, co-writing four of the seven new songs. Tackett co-wrote the rest: two with Barrère and one with Payne.

Like every album since *Representing the Mambo*, *Chinese Work Songs* mixes genres in a delightful Feats gumbo – or, as Barrère put it in the liner notes: 'another incredible opus, mixing several bags of musical stylings thrown together in a Chinese herbologists mortar, and ground into aural acupuncture.'

Released in June 2000, *Chinese Work Songs* failed to chart. But what mattered to the band was performing the new songs live, and that was where the grassroots campaign hit its stride. The band performed 115 shows over the year, the most since 1995 when they were struggling to fill venues. But thanks to the power of the internet, more and more fans were connecting with the band to find out the latest news directly from the source. Additionally, *Chinese Work Songs* – like its predecessor – was sold at concerts, often selling more than 50 copies a night: far exceeding the number in local stores. Management had initially balked at this tactic, but Payne argued, 'What, it's only reserved for country artists?'

With their confidence at an all-time high, but weary of bouncing from label to label, the band decided to set up their own label Hot Tomato Records. Payne said in the official statement: 'It's something we've talked about doing for a long time. It gives us the chance to do what we want, and it's there for everybody in the band ... and when it's really up and running, for other artists too.' The inaugural releases were *Raw Tomatos* and *Ripe Tomatos* – double-disc compilations of select live Little Feat performances from 1971 to 2001, with the occasional home demo or onstage jam thrown in for good measure.

Having their own label, finally gave the band the control they deserved, not only over their future studio output but also their live output – after all, their concerts had gotten the grassroots movement moving in the first place. For just over a decade, Hot Tomato Records served as Little Feat's home, releasing seven contemporaneous live albums, three studio albums and the occasional solo album: not bad for a band who'd consistently flown under the radar for the better part of 30 years.

'Rag Mama Rag' (Robbie Robertson)
Little Feat's glorious ramshackle cover of The Band's 'Rag Mama Rag' – originally from their eponymous 1969 album – retains the spirit of the

original without coming off too polished, contrived, or contemporary. Barrère takes the lead vocal while Murphy harmonizes superbly. Gradney does his best to approximate the original's bottom end, on bass instead of tuba, and pianist Payne channels his inner Garth Hudson. But they can't help extemporizing on a good groove, even if it means dragging the song out longer than it should've been.

'Eula' (Paul Barrère, Fred Tackett)
Whenever Barrère and Tackett wrote together, the results were always a delightful surprise; a little left-field but still embodying the spirit of both Little Feat and the writers. 'Eula' – their fourth collaboration – tells the story of a young teacher getting up to no good with a boy from Mississippi. Set to a boozy, plodding rhythm, it features the songwriters dueling on dobros with Payne on piano, before ending abruptly with a messy stutter.

'Bed Of Roses' (Shaun Murphy, Bill Payne)
Murphy takes the lead on this track which sets off straight out of the gate and never lets up. Barrère is right alongside her on bottleneck guitar: answering her every line about a hard-worn woman born under a bad sign, with a swoop down the fretboard. The band's enthusiasm is palpable, and they turn what could've been a conventional boogie rocker into a true barnstormer.

'Sample In A Jar' (Trey Anastasio, Tom Marshall)
In the past, it wasn't uncommon for Little Feat to cover songs by contemporary artists (Allen Toussaint's 'On Your Way Down' was released only a year before Little Feat's version on *Dixie Chicken*), but what *was* uncommon was them covering a song by a band 20 years their junior, who had cited them as an influence. Payne recalled the confusion over the lineage to Dean Budnick on jambands.com: 'At one point, Paul had said that Phish covers 'On Your Way Down', but I said, 'So are we doing them doing us doing them?', and Paul was laughing. Then Paul played me 'Sample In A Jar,' and I said, 'That's the tune.''

A grassroots organization of Phish fans approached Little Feat to record a song for the Mockingbird Foundation (mbird.org). Payne and Barrère jumped at the opportunity, finally recording the song at the tail end of the sessions. Payne explained to Budnick: 'So we made a quick chart of it, ran it down a couple times and recorded it. When we listened to it back, Paul and I looked at each other and said, 'We have to record another song for the charity, because this one has to go on our record.''

Compared to Phish's original, Little Feat slows the tempo ever so slightly, with the guitar riff mutated into an approximation of Hendrix's 'Hey Joe'; Payne's Hammond giving a summery, late-1960s psychedelic feel. Barrère especially lets loose with several scorching guitar solos, clearly relishing in the ability to be just a little unhinged. While Little Feat *did* release the song on *Chinese Work Songs*, in July 2001, it also ended up on *Sharin' in the Groove:*

Celebrating the Music of Phish – one of the fastest-selling tribute albums ever: over 25,000 in the first two weeks.

'Just Another Sunday' (Shaun Murphy, Bill Payne)

This sprawling epic fuses jazz with worldbeat, with a guitar riff reminiscent of Paul Simon's 'Under African Skies.' Payne takes the lead vocal on the first two verses, where he takes a walk down memory lane, returning to his old neighborhood, before running into a fortune teller. Murphy then takes over, casting visions of the future while urging Payne to change his reckless abandon. The song is a testament to the talents of not only the band – who pull off the masterful and precise eight-minute arrangement with ease – but to Payne and Murphy as songwriters. The track is not just the highlight of *Chinese Work Songs*, but is a bona fide latter-day classic.

'Gimme A Stone' (David Forman, Eric Bazilian, Rick Chertoff, Rob Hyman)

In 1998, producer Rick Chertoff and The Hooters founding member Rob Hyman (former college roommates) teamed up on *Largo*: an Americana music project loosely based on Dvořák's *New World Symphony* (its second movement providing the project title). The project was released as an album in April 1998, featuring Taj Mahal, Levon Helm, Garth Hudson, Joan Osborne, Cyndi Lauper and The Chieftains. With such an impressive roster, it's astonishing that the album flopped (*AllMusic*'s Geoff Ginsberg equating it to hitting 'a home run while the entire crowd was out in the beer line.')

When it came time to select material for the new album, Hayward suggested covering 'Gimme A Stone', and when takes with Murphy and Barrère singing lead failed to pass muster, Payne suggested Hayward sing his first lead vocal on a Little Feat song. 'We just looked at Richie and said, 'You know, this will fit your voice',' Payne told Dean Budnick of jambands.com. 'It's like a Holy Modal Rounders tune, and Richie always sounded like the Holy Modal Rounders to me.'

While the amount of covers on *Chinese Work Songs* was unusually high, the quality of the performances is unquestioned – none overshadow the originals, but are all worthy contenders, with 'Gimme A Stone' ranking among the band's finest.

'Rio Esperanza' (Bill Payne, Shaun Murphy)

The band slows things down with this gorgeous acoustic ballad, starting off with just Payne and Murphy on piano and vocal – the latter singing poignantly of star-crossed lovers separated by geography. Verse by verse, an instrument is added: first a wheezing accordion, then a chiming mandolin, upright bass, and finally, a light acoustic guitar. The performance has a wistful, melancholy air. It's a superb but forgotten composition – Murphy certainly had affection for it, recording it again for her 2010 solo album *Trouble With Lovin'*.

'Tattoo Heart' (Paul Barrère, Shaun Murphy)

Clayton and Hayward are all over this, locking into a gentle groove that's adorned with mystical-sounding percussion from Lenny Castro and Piero Mariani. Murphy again channels the spirits of New Orleans on this dark and moody piece.

'Marginal Creatures' (Fred Tackett, Paul Barrère)

It would be easy to write off 'Marginal Creatures' as a conventional rocker, except there's really no such thing in Little Feat's discography. Besides, the little touches of Barrère's scorching bottleneck, Payne's Hammond and Murphy's backing vocals, are distinctive and definitive Little Feat. Sure, the song turns into an excuse for Barrère and Tackett to trade guitar licks, but who cares – the band is having a blast.

'Chinese Work Songs' (Bill Payne, Fred Tackett)

The title track takes the everything-and-the-kitchen-sink approach, with Payne and Tackett throwing every musical twist and genre shift they can think of at an outsider's story of traveling in a foreign land. There's little wrong with the track, though it strays uncomfortably close to cliche with the eastern-inspired mid-song interjection, which is rife with chanting and samples of percussion and traditional Chinese instruments.

But for the most part, the song is a scorching rocker, with Barrère spitting out the lyrics in a cadence comparable only to Van Halen's David Lee Roth; in fact, as ludicrous as it sounds, this could pass as an outtake from the early Van Halen days. Joe Sublett and Darrell Leonard add brass blasts throughout, the former trading riffs with Payne's Hammond halfway through, before getting the spotlight at the song's close: his unrestrained solo matched only by Barrère's equally-raucous fretwork. Apart from a few minor lapses in judgment, 'Chinese Work Songs' is a carefree, freewheelin' rocker with a sense of humor that positively cooks.

'It Takes A Lot To Laugh, It Takes A Train to Cry' (Bob Dylan)

The album closes with this slow-as-molasses cover of Bob Dylan's blues workout from 1965's *Highway 61 Revisited*. Murphy introduced the song to the band's repertoire in 1999. After her departure in 2009, she revisited the song – along with two tracks from Feat's *Ain't Had Enough Fun* ('That's A Pretty Good Love' and 'Rock And Roll Everynight') on her debut solo album *Livin' the Blues*.

Kickin' It At the Barn (2003)

Personnel:
Paul Barrère: guitars, vocals, dobro, lead vocals except as noted
Sam Clayton: percussion, vocals
Kenny Gradney: bass
Richie Hayward: drums, vocals
Shaun Murphy: vocals, hand percussion; co-lead vocal on 'Corazones Y Sombras';
lead vocal on 'I'd Be Lyin''
Bill Payne: keyboards, vocals; co-lead vocal on 'Corazones Y Sombras'; lead vocal
on 'Fighting The Mosquito Wars'
Fred Tackett: electric guitar, vocals, dobro, mandolin, mandocello, trumpet; lead
vocal on 'In A Town Like This'
Additional personnel:
Larry Campbell: violin on 'Night On The Town' and 'Bill's River Blues'
Nacho Hernandez: accordion on 'Corazones Y Sombras'
Gabriel Gonzales: co-lead vocal on 'Corazones Y Sombras'
Sergio 'Checo' Alonso: arpa jalisciense on 'Corazones Y Sombras'
Jesus 'Chuy' Guzman: trumpet, mellophone on 'Corazones Y Sombras'
Piero Mariani: percussion on 'Corazones Y Sombras,' 'Stomp' and 'Fighting The
Mosquito Wars'
Recorded at The Barn and Love Tribe Studios, Topanga, January-June 2003
Producers: Paul Barrère, Bill Payne and Fred Tackett
Release date: US: 21 October 2003
Peak position: US: -
Running time: 71:27

Having established Hot Tomato Records as a viable home for live albums, it
was now time to record the label's first studio album. In January 2003, Barrère
joined Tackett at his barn ('More like a big shed,' Hayward clarified) in Topanga
Canyon for informal songwriting sessions. This yielded three co-writes – 'Night
On The Town,' 'Heaven Forsaken' and 'Why Don't It Look Like The Way That
It Talk' – before Payne and Murphy joined them in February when most of
the remaining songs were written. Murphy's 'I'd Be Lyin'' (written with her
husband Piero Mariani and friend Laura Creamer) and Tackett's 'In A Town
Like This' (from his 2003 debut solo album of the same title) were brought
in already prepared; Payne's 'Stomp' had started life during the *Chinese
Work Songs* sessions, and 'Fighting The Mosquito Wars' was from an earlier,
unrealized Payne project.

The initial plan was to again record at home (Barrère's: by now re-
christened Each Hit Studios), but necessary repairs forced a relocation.
Tackett offered up his barn again, so Jerry Manuel, Roger Cole and Denny
Jones transferred the recording equipment, setting it up at Tackett's. Ken
Lloyd and Jaime Scher built a usable studio space while the band was
recording. So there were frequent interruptions – the album recorded

piecemeal between April and June 2003, with the band squeezing in tour dates when they could. Barrère wrote in the liner notes: 'Somehow, between touring and recording, we got it all together.'

They sure did. Despite external chaos, this album is warm, cozy and comfortable – not in the sense that it's safe or conventional, but that you actually feel like you're in the barn with the band and they're playing directly to you. There is the occasional scene change ('Fighting The Mosquito Wars' sounds like it was performed in a meadow outside at sunrise, and 'Corazones Y Sombras' jumps from the kitchen to south of the border, to the dance floor), but this is an intimate, personal recording.

Never one to get overly sentimental in album liner notes, Barrère waxed poetically on the sessions: 'This has been truly one of the most memorable recording projects we've done,' he began, before offering up session memories. But he couldn't praise the chemistry enough, gushing, 'We just seemed to click on all cylinders.'

With recording finished by June and the album mixed by August, the band embarked on an all-acoustic tour (a handful of electric dates were interspersed in the summer and fall), inspired by Barrère and Tackett's successful 1999 acoustic duo concerts. Payne told Mick Skidmore on jambands.com that this was deliberate: 'When we did this record, I said to Paul ahead of time, 'I think we ought to make a record that is acoustic in nature.' – meaning a record where we are not worried about writing rockers per se: those will come out on their own. I said, 'Let's write a folk song.' I'd never written a folk song.' The new approach translated well to the more intimate live setting – the new songs blending well with the rearranged acoustic favorites.

Released in October 2003, *Kickin' It at the Barn* failed to chart (no surprise there), but did earn warm reviews. AllMusic's Stephen Thomas Erlewine praised the first two songs as 'first-rate, and the moody 'Why Don't It Look Like The Way That It Talk' isn't far behind either. Like much reunited Little Feat, (the album) is a little too laid-back and groove-centric for its own good, but there's a better variety of grooves, sounds and songs on this: enough to make it one of their stronger latter-day affairs.'

C. Michael Bailey concluded his gushing review on allaboutjazz.com with '*Kickin' It* marks an exciting time for Little Feat, whose creativity and muse continues to grow. Highly recommended.'

Indeed: *Kickin' It* is one of the band's finest albums and has a warm, earthy feel. The production and mix are the most organic a Little Feat record has ever been. (No surprise then that a 5.1 DVD-A mix (by engineer Gilberto Morales) was released for audiophiles.) The band sounds completely at ease with each other, which Barrère noted in the liners: 'If music is a conversation between the players, then we are talking like never before.' It's their longest studio album by nearly a minute, beating out the previous record-breaker *Under the Radar*, but it never overstays its welcome – even if some tracks could've benefited from light editing; then again, why cut off a band, mid-conversation?

'Night On The Town' (Fred Tackett, Paul Barrère)

The album lives up to its title with this solid countrified rocker, featuring a soulful backing vocal, dobro and violin from Larry Campbell. Barrère has a ball with the lyrics, looking forward to the weekend when he can spend time with his junkyard friends and escape a nagging wife and workplace responsibilities: 'Eat, drink and be merry/A man has to have a reason to live.' As with most of the album's songs, this has an extended outro – the last two minutes allowing the band to stretch out and let loose. Payne's solo is rollicking fun, while the final, wistful vamp he introduces as the song ends is especially pleasant.

'Heaven Forsaken' (Fred Tackett, Paul Barrère)

In a fair and just world, 'Heaven Forsaken' would've been the album's late-summer radio hit, but it wasn't to be for this fine mid-tempo rocker. The song marries a bluesy verse structure to a gospel-tinged chorus – that wouldn't have been out of place on any latter-day Rolling Stones album, though Barrère's singing is no match for Mick Jagger's.

'I'd Be Lyin'' (Laura Creamer, Piero Mariani, Shaun Murphy)

While on tour with Bob Seger in the 1990s, Murphy and fellow backing singer and friend Laura Creamer started writing a song together but abandoned it before it could progress beyond the first verse. Several years later, Murphy and her husband Piero Mariani set up a home studio, set the words to music and fleshed out the arrangement, ending up with 'I'd Be Lyin''. Murphy and Mariani mix a vague reggae feel with a moody New Orleans-inspired blues; some introductory *audio vérité* of waves breaking, adding to the atmosphere.

'Corazones Y Sombras' (Bill Payne, Michael Donnelly, Paul Barrère, Stephen Bruton)

Not only the album highlight, but the highlight of Little Feat's latter-day catalog, 'Corazones Y Sombras' ('Hearts And Shadows') is an eight-minute epic instigated by Payne, with assistance from Barrère and songwriter friend Stephen Bruton (Spanish translation by Michael Donnelly). This cinematic Tex-Mex *tour de force* is a testament not only to Payne's love of Mexico but to his maturity as a songwriter, arranger and singer. The band too push their limits, with Hayward especially shining on the various rhythmic shifts. Payne was later justifiably proud of the composition, devoting two pages of liner notes to its inception and all involved in its creation: 'It is often difficult to pinpoint where the journey starts. A blend of impulse, intuition, influences, studied direction, conversation, immersion all play their part in summoning the courage to act upon something you don't quite understand.'

'Walking As Two' (Bill Payne, Fred Tackett, Paul Barrère, Shaun Murphy)

The fiesta mood mellows on this moody, atmospheric piece, with Barrère singing the somber lyrics of the passage of time and remaining married: not out of bliss but out of duty. (The similarity to the 'Old Folks Boogie' melody is a delightfully-subtle self-reference.) Payne's electric piano gives the song a cool, jazz-like feel, and Barrère's tasteful guitar solo is beautiful in its simplicity: making this an undisputed album highlight.

'In A Town Like This' (Fred Tackett)

Tackett and Barrère had already penned a handful of songs in their pre-album writing sessions, but Tackett gets his first solo credit and lead vocal on this song, written for and released on his 2003 debut solo album of the same name. Here it's given a full electric arrangement, which – in talking to his local paper *The Topanga Messenger* in January 2004 – Tackett equated as 'Little Feat doing a Paul Butterfield Blues Band screaming electric version of this blues song.' Tackett is a capable vocalist (one has to wonder why the band waited so long to give him a spotlight), delivering the rather purple lines ('The highway running serpentine through canebrake and maple/Reluctantly relinquishing to hardwood and pine') with the droll, tongue-in-cheek approach that only he could provide.

'Fighting The Mosquito Wars' (Bill Payne)

The first of two Payne compositions, this song dated from 'a previous thing I had done a couple of years before.' That 'previous thing' was a 20 November 1999 house concert – specifically at the house of Russ and Julie Paris of Oak Park, California – where he performed a mixture of poetry, recent Little Feat songs, including ones that ended up on *Chinese Work Songs*, and this song.

Payne is in a reflective mood, with lines like 'The sun setting off of her smile/It was pure magic' and 'I'll see you on the other side someday' recalling a simpler time. The arrangement evokes a late summer's night with its languid pace, shimmering guitar work and gentle, brushed drums, interrupted only by a mid-song diversion into a raga-inspired jam: 'We knew where it was going to begin, but we didn't know where it was going to end, so it was a question of just listening to how the people were playing,' Barrère told triblive.com, suggesting that the recording was captured live. 'It became evident this was winding down and then we were going to get back into the feel of the song. The passages in between the different sections were as smooth as can be, and that has to do with the fact that we have been playing together for a long, long time.'

'Stomp' (Bill Payne)

'That's the song that got the police called on us,' Tackett told his local paper *The Topanga Messenger* in January 2004. 'It's a raging instrumental piece: very fast, loud and viciously complicated. It took us two days of six to seven hours per day, full-bore, to get it down. It's ten minutes long and wild the whole time.'

'Stomp' began life during sessions for *Chinese Work Songs*, but it hadn't gelled, so was put aside. But Payne was determined to make it work this time. It's little more than an excuse for the band to jam, but their enthusiasm is so palpable, the groove so infectious and the extemporizing so exciting, that the nine-minute running time still somehow feels too short.

Not everyone felt that way – during one of the performances, Barrère called an abrupt halt to inform Tackett that an officer was on scene. Tackett told *The Topanga Messenger*: 'He was investigating a neighbor's complaint about the loud music. When the officer asked who we were, Richie sang the 'Dixie Chicken' line, and the officer instantly knew.' Tackett's wife Patricia added, 'We patched things up with the neighbor, sent her flowers, and assured her that they would be finished recording soon,' to which Tackett countered, 'I don't blame her. Once she knew who it was, she was okay with it. We appreciate her cooperation, but we really have to soundproof this place so nobody will care.'

'Why Don't It Look Like The Way That It Talk' (Fred Tackett, Paul Barrère)
Despite its folky guitar intro, this song is a laid-back, jazz-like affair, with Barrère singing a verbose, absurdist lament of things not appearing to be what they should. A shade under eight minutes long, it takes its time in unfolding, but it's the little things that maintain interest – whether it's Tackett's trumpet or mandolin or Payne's cool electric piano performance. The most poignant part comes from Barrère – a survivor then at the age of 53 – singing, 'It's good to be alive, yeah, so good to be alive': delivered defiantly like a mission statement in a moment of lucidity.

'I Do What The Telephone Tells Me To Do' (Bill Payne, Fred Tackett, Paul Barrère)
Another Barrère-sung boogie rocker, this slinky extended jam was derived from a jam he incorporated into contemporary 'Dixie Chicken' performances. He told triblive.com: 'And then, we're going to take a song that (Payne) had started to write years ago, but I thought could fit into this song. Billy wrote another section we added to the middle of it. It was then just a question of writing the lyrics, showing it to the guys and saying, 'OK, here's where the different movements take place. We'll just make all these transitions, and it should be swinging.' And it wound up swinging.'

'Bill's River Blues' (Bill Payne, Paul Barrère)
The album closes with this gentle Payne poem, set to music initiated by Barrère after Payne suggested they write a folk song. Payne told jambands.com: 'I was just throwing imagery down, and Paul came up with some of his own, so he threw in a line or two. It was born out of an idea that was stabilized by the fact that we had some lyrics to go to, and we took it from there. We literally sat across from each other, I at the piano and him with the guitar, and worked

it out.' That intimate simplicity carried over to the final recording, with Payne and Barrère the only Feats on the track (Larry Campbell guests on violin); the others having packed up and left hours ago – these two old friends getting one more song out of each other before finally heading home.

Join the Band (2008)

Personnel:
Paul Barrère: guitar, vocals
Sam Clayton: percussion, vocals
Kenny Gradney: bass
Richie Hayward: drums, vocals
Shaun Murphy: vocals
Bill Payne: keyboards, vocals
Fred Tackett: guitar, mandolin, trumpet, vocals
Lead vocals and additional personnel noted below individual songs.
Recorded at Shrimpboat Sound Studios, Key West; Ocean Way, Hollywood
('Trouble'); La La Land Studios, Sheffield; Ocean Way, Nashville; Omni Sound
Studios, Nashville
Producers: Bill Payne, Mac McAnally
Executive producer: Jimmy Buffett
Release date: US: 1 July 2008
Peak position: US: 81
Running time: 62:48

Payne had been keen on the idea of a special recording project – Little Feat joined by guest vocalists and musicians – for Jimmy Buffett's label Mailboat Records. But communication between the band's and Buffett's management had broken down. Desperate to make it work, Payne contacted Buffett independently (which led to Payne guesting on Buffett's 2003 album *License to Chill*: Buffett's first, and to date, only number-1 album) and they finally got to discuss the idea further.

Payne describes the long process from idea to finished product in greater detail in the liner notes. In short, sessions started at Buffett's Shrimpboat Sound Studios in Key West in autumn 2005, with overdubs recorded at Mac McAnally's La La Land Studios in Sheffield, Alabama (home of the famed Muscle Shoals Sound Studio). Additional sessions took place at Nashville's Ocean Way and Omni Sound, with 'Trouble' recorded at Ocean Way in Hollywood, which Payne humbly noted brought their career full circle.

Most of the guest vocalist choices were no-brainers (Bob Seger, Emmylou Harris, Craig Fuller and Buffett himself), while some of the more unusual choices (Dave Matthews, Brooks and Dunn and the Black Crowes' Chris Robinson) were bold and surprising. Robinson was invited because Buffett's production coordinator Heikki Larsen and his daughter Savannah were at a Black Crowes concert where they played 'Willin'' in their encore. A chuffed Payne called Robinson the next day and asked him to sing on 'Oh Atlanta.' (Brooks and Dunn had already been reserved for 'Willin'', though one wishes he'd made an exception.) Non-vocal guests included members of Buffett's Coral Reefer Band (Mike Utley, Robert Greenidge, Ralph MacDonald and Jim Mayer), Brad Paisley, Sam Bush, Sonny Landreth and Phish's Mike Gordon, with Béla Fleck making his second appearance on a Little Feat record.

Join the Band sounds like a bunch of musician friends stopping by for a quick jam session, stepping in and out as needed. There are no surprises: the Little Feat songs are all safe choices, while some of the covers are adventurous – especially the gorgeous Barrère/Buffett duet 'Champion Of The World' and Barrère, Murphy and Clayton's downright fun vocal ping-ponging on 'Don't You Just Know It.' The undisputed highlight is Inara George – by now a musician in her own right and half of indie outfit The Bird and the Bee – who sang her father's gorgeous 'Trouble': written for her mother Liz, who used to sing it to her as a lullaby.

Join the Band is a pleasant diversion – a unique way to honor Little Feat's past and also have a good time. But it was a disappointing follow-up to *Kickin' It at the Barn*. It also broke the longest drought since their reunion – five years between studio albums, with another four passing before the next.

There were a few personnel changes in those intervening years – Shaun Murphy departed shortly after the album's release: on good terms and under the auspices of starting a solo career. While she did indeed do just that (to date, she's released eight albums), her departure was a little more nuanced. Certain fans had never fully warmed to her, and while she had started strong on *Ain't Had Enough Fun*, her presence over subsequent albums had diminished, with Barrère and Payne taking on more lead vocals. Tellingly, Murphy submitted lyrics for three or four songs on *Kickin' It*, all of which were rejected ('I'd Be Lyin'' was recorded at the last minute), which only hastened her eventual departure.

The clincher was when Murphy had to beg off from a tour due to prior commitments with Bob Seger. Little Feat's new management witnessed a show without Murphy. After attending one with her back in the fold, they asked Barrère and Payne what exactly she added to the lineup anymore. (Plus, having one less permanent member made more financial sense.) A band meeting (minus Murphy) was held, a consensus decided, and Murphy was informed. She has remained appreciative of her time with the band, and diplomatic in her dismissal, refusing to say a bad word against them.

The other drastic personnel change came on 12 August 2010, when the band's idiosyncratic drummer of over 40 years – Richie Hayward – died from complications of a lung disease while awaiting a liver transplant. On the *Little Feat Radio Hour*, Hayward described himself and the first incarnation of the band as 'pharmacological test pilots,' and never made any excuses for his lifestyle. Sadly, it simply caught up with him, and he was diagnosed with liver cancer in mid-2009. While on the road promoting *Join the Band*, Hayward informed the others that his last show would be on 7 August in Billings, Montana, as he needed time off to fight the disease. His drum tech Gabe Ford filled in, ostensibly until Hayward's return.

On 11 July 2010 at the Vancouver Island MusicFest, Hayward returned to the stage with Little Feat one final time. Shortly after his diagnosis, he and his Canadian wife Shauna had moved there, but Hayward didn't qualify for state medical treatment and didn't have medical insurance. (Payne helped, setting up benefit concerts and auctions, with Hayward's wife using the band website to keep fans updated on the drummer's developments.) With Hayward now too ill to play, the band invited him to watch from the wings. But Barrère coaxed him out to sing the Jamaican national anthem 'Jamaica, Land We Love,' before Hayward took to the drum stool to finish 'Willin'', then playing 'Spanish Moon,' 'Skin It Back' and 'Fat Man In The Bathtub.'

Hayward's death served as an impetus for the band to continue but also as a reminder of their own mortality. They were approaching retirement age but simply had no desire to do so. They did temper their rigorous schedule, but only so much – in 2011, they played a total of 76 shows (five more than in 2009), though each successive year's number of concerts diminished. But that wasn't due to a lack of desire or demand, but to yet another health issue rearing its ugly head: this time for Barrère, as a result of one part of Hayward's 'pharmacological test pilots.'

'Fat Man In The Bathtub' (Lowell George)
Dave Matthews: vocal; Sonny Landreth: slide guitar and solo; Mac McAnally: National guitar

Little Feat turn down the urgency and immediacy on this dreamy reworking of the *Dixie Chicken* favorite, with Dave Matthews acquitting himself well, despite his mush-mouthed approach being completely at odds with Lowell George's gritty, tongue-in-cheek delivery. The track meanders in the middle, with the band jamming a bit aimlessly, though Sonny Landreth's lovely bottleneck solo is worth it. But as an opener, 'Fat Man' just doesn't work – European editions swapped it with 'Dixie Chicken': a far more effective choice.

'Something In The Water' (Al Anderson, Jeffrey Steele, Bob DiPiero)
Bob Seger: vocal; Brad Paisley: lead guitar; McAnally: backing vocals; Sam Bush: fiddle

First recorded by Jeffrey Steele, this features Bob Seger and Brad Paisley. While the musicians are undoubtedly having a blast, Seger's vocal is a little too shouty, and the twangy C&W sound, grates.

'Dixie Chicken' (Lowell George, Fred Martin)
Vince Gill: vocal; McAnally: acoustic guitar, backing vocals; Landreth: slide guitar; Michael Utley: Hammond organ; Ralph McDonald: shaker

Vince Gill over-sings on this otherwise faithful arrangement of the 1973 favorite.

123

'See You Later Alligator' (Robert Guidry)
Barrère and Murphy: vocals; McAnally: acoustic guitar, backing vocals; Utley: Hammond; Jim Mayer: slap and double bass

Barrère and Murphy team up, especially letting loose for this spirited cover – first recorded by Cajun singer-songwriter Bobby Charles in 1955 but made popular the following year by Bill Haley and His Comets.

'Champion Of The World' (Will Kimbrough, Gwil Owen)
Jimmy Buffett with Barrère: vocals; McAnally: acoustic and high-strung guitars

Barrère and Buffett swap verses on this lovely acoustic ballad, first recorded by co-writer Will Kimbrough on his 2002 album *Home Away*. Payne's Hammond solo is sublime.

'The Weight' (Robbie Robertson)
Barrère: vocal; McAnally: acoustic guitar; Utley: Hammond; Béla Fleck: banjo

While nothing can ever beat the round-the-campfire arrangement of The Band's original, this is still a good cover, even if the tempo is taken a bit too quick and Hayward's flashy drumming is more of a distraction than an enhancement.

'Don't You Just Know It' (Huey 'Piano' Smith)
Barrère, Clayton, and Murphy: vocals; McAnally: tic-tac tele

First released by its songwriter in January 1958, this is a fun call-and-response between the band and whichever vocalist is taking the lead – whether it's Murphy's raucous wailing, Clayton's *basso profundo* growling or Barrère's nasal sneer.

'Time Loves A Hero' (Paul Barrère, Kenny Gradney, Bill Payne)
Buffett with Payne: vocals; McAnally: backing vocals; Tackett: electric guitar with a pencil; Utley: Hammond; MacDonald: tamborine, cowbell; Robert Greenidge: pans

Buffett and most of the Coral Reefer Band stop by for this largely faithful rendition of Buffett's favorite Little Feat song, and one he opened his set with on 17 February 2005. Payne sings the occasional line and as backup, but this is mostly Buffett's show. Subtle touches like Robert Greenidge's steel drums and Tackett's guitar played with a pencil, are nice.

'Willin'' (Lowell George)
Ronnie Dunn and Kicks Brooks: vocals; McAnally: electric and acoustic guitars, Hammond, backing vocal; McDonald: tamborine, triangle; Duncan Cameron: pedal steel

If weepy, twangy C&W pop is your thing, then you'll love this.

'This Land Is Your Land' (Woody Guthrie)
Barrère and Murphy: vocals; McAnally: acoustic guitar, backing vocal; Utley: Hammond, backing vocal; Alan Schulman: backing vocal; Mike Gordon: bass

The world wasn't exactly waiting for Little Feat to tackle Woody Guthrie's sardonic criticism of nationalism disguised as patriotism, but this isn't bad. Barrère plays up the sarcasm while Murphy counters it with her leonine vocal roar.

'Oh Atlanta' (Bill Payne)
Chris Robinson with Payne: vocals; McAnally: acoustic guitar, backing vocal

The Black Crowes' Chris Robinson stops by to trade lines and harmonize with Payne, though Robinson's rock-god howl grates against the latter's more mellow delivery. Otherwise, the arrangement is largely unchanged.

'Spanish Moon' (Lowell George)
Clayton with Craig Fuller: vocals; McAnally: acoustic guitar; Vince Gill: acoustic guitar solo

After fifteen years, Fuller returns on this scorching and superb duet with Clayton. Vince Gill offers a tasteful acoustic guitar solo while Hayward and Gradney keep the groove going – though why Payne didn't ask Robert Greenidge to play steel drums instead of them being approximated on keyboards – is anyone's guess.

'Trouble' (Lowell George)
Inara George: lead vocal

The best was saved for second-to-last. Featuring only Payne on piano and Lowell George's daughter Inara singing, this performance is superb, sublime and every other superlative that can be thrown at it. While Inara has carved out her own distinctive sound and identity (her back catalog is well worth checking out on its own merits), there's still something magical in hearing her sing her father's words – words he had written for his wife and Inara's mother, Liz.

'Sailin' Shoes' (Lowell George)
Emmylou Harris, Murphy and Barrère: vocals; McAnally: National guitar, backing vocal; Bush: fiddle, mandolin; Fleck: banjo

Emmylou Harris returns for her first Little Feat album appearance since 1974. The arrangement doesn't try to match that of the original (nothing could compare to that spontaneous, ramshackle performance), but instead more closely follows the live arrangement – until halfway through, when the song kicks into high gear, borrowing an arrangement from Sam Bush that turns it into a raucous rave-up and a perfect album closer.

Related track
'I Will Play For Gumbo' (Jimmy Buffett)
Barrère: vocal; Bush: fiddle

Barrère takes the lead, and Sam Bush saws away on fiddle for this spirited Jimmy Buffett cover: an up-tempo rocker from 1999's *Beach House on the Moon*. Why the song was consigned to bonus track status is a mystery – there's plenty of room on the album, and the song is certainly a better choice than some of the other covers.

Rooster Rag (2012)

Personnel:

Paul Barrère: guitars, slide guitar, vocals; lead vocal on 'Candyman Blues,' 'Just A Fever' and 'Jamaica Will Break Your Heart'; co-lead vocal on 'One Breath At A Time'

Sam Clayton: congas, vocals; lead vocal on 'Mellow Down Easy'; co-lead vocal on 'One Breath At A Time'

Gabe Ford: drums, vocals

Kenny Gradney: bass

Bill Payne: keyboards, vocals; lead vocal on 'Rooster Rag,' 'Rag Top Down,' 'Way Down Under,' 'Salome' and 'The Blues Keep Coming'

Fred Tackett: guitar, vocals, mandolin; lead vocal on 'Church Falling Down' and 'Tattooed Girl'; co-lead vocal on 'One Breath At A Time'

Additional personnel:

Larry Campbell: fiddle on 'Rooster Rag' and 'Salome'

The Texicali Horns (Joe Sublett: saxophone; Darrell Leonard: trumpet) on 'Jamaica Will Break Your Heart' and 'One Breath At A Time'

Kim Wilson: harmonica on 'Mellow Down Easy'

Johnny Lee Schell: guitar, vocal

Recorded at Ultratone Studios, Studio City

Producers: Paul Barrère, Bill Payne

Release date: US: 26 June 2012

Peak position: US: 160

Running time: 57:56

Not counting *Join the Band*, it had been nine years since Little Feat's last album: a time span matched only by that between *Down on the Farm* and *Let It Roll*. But it wasn't for lack of trying: Payne had gone through another period of writer's block, admitting he'd been unable to finish a song on his own since his 2005 solo album *Cielo Norte*. So the idea to record an all-blues-covers album was proposed. A handful of songs were recorded in February 2011, before the project was abandoned entirely (only 'Candyman Blues' and 'Mellow Down Easy' made the final record).

Perhaps there just wasn't as much urgency to write and record a new album. Little Feat records had never been big sellers, and the musical landscape had shifted drastically by 2012. Additionally, the band's label Hot Tomato Records had largely run its course (with a series of live archival releases to its name, along with Tackett and Payne's solo projects). The new album *was* released on the label but distributed through Rounder Records, and would be the final Hot Tomato release.

Besides, there had been other distractions – In 2003, the Annual Featfan Fest was established, which eventually morphed into the Ramble on the Island, in the Jamaican resort town of Negril, with the band performing full sets and occasional solo or duet shows with guests, for a couple of hundred fans. And, of course, there had been the devastating news of Hayward's death in 2010.

But the band's future as a live act was never in doubt. It was simply a matter of whether writing and recording an album would be worth it.

What helped get the album in motion was a writing collaboration that was both surprising and a no-brainer: Former Grateful Dead manager Cameron Sears and Little Feat's new manager simply asked Payne if he and Barrère would be interested in working with Jerry Garcia's lyricist of choice Robert Hunter. Both jumped at the chance, though a collaboration with Barrère fizzled out. He told *Marquee Magazine* in 2012:

I sent Robert a track that I was working on called 'Scuffle The Shuffle,' and told him I had some lyrics I had already been working on. He replied with a whole slew of lyrics of his own. I wrote back saying, 'Some of these are really great. Do you mind if I kind of pick and choose and put them together with the lyrics I got?' But he really wanted to have his whole lyric intact.

Only one of Barrère's songs – 'Just A Fever,' co-written with Stephen Bruton – ended up on the album: the least amount of original material Barrère had contributed to a Little Feat album since *Dixie Chicken*.

But Payne had found a sympathetic ear in Hunter. The fruitful collaboration yielded a total of ten songs, with four released on the eventual album. What was strange about the process was that it was done entirely over the internet. Payne told dead.net:

We've never spoken on the phone. I Googled his picture to see what he looks like! So far, it's all been over the internet. Robert is a very private guy, and I don't sit there and analyze his lyrics. But what I did with all this freedom I was given to write with him, I'd sit there and figure, 'Well, this is obviously a chorus, that's great. And this looks like a B section or maybe a bridge,' and I'd start working things out.

While the entire album could've consisted of Payne/Hunter co-writes, room was made for Tackett, who contributed four songs and sang lead on two. Clayton also sang lead on 'Mellow Down Easy' – his first full vocal on a Feats album since *Down on the Farm* – and sang with Tackett and Barrère on the breezy 'One Breath At A Time.'

Rehearsed and recorded quickly at Johnny Lee Schell's Ultratone Studios over two months at the start of 2012, *Rooster Rag* marked the debut of Gabe Ford as Little Feat's drummer: a position he would hold until 2020. Clayton told Ben Fong-Torres: 'It's easier to play with Gabe, because Gabe is thinking along my lines … (he) plays more funk, more straight-ahead.' Ford is not as flashy as Hayward was, but his approach suited the new songs. Besides, he'd earned his place, having risen to the challenge of replacing the irreplaceable Hayward. So he deserved a role on a new record and even co-wrote 'The Blues Keep Coming' with Payne.

Released in June 2012, *Rooster Rag* revitalized Little Feat, and the overwhelmingly positive response floored them. Payne gushed to Fong-Torres: 'I felt we'd hit a real home run. I haven't heard that kind of thing since *Let It Roll*.'

But the momentum was cut short. When the tour finished up in March 2013, Paul Barrère had to take a leave of absence to focus on treatments for Hepatitis C. 'For the past 20 years, I have managed to control the effects of the disease with lifestyle changes and the love and support of my family and friends,' he explained on the band's website, before optimistically concluding, 'Music is my life, and I still have plenty left in me that I plan on sharing.'

'Candyman Blues' (Mississippi John Hurt)

This raucous blues rocker had been a live favorite since 2004 when it was tagged onto the end of 'Down On The Farm.' But it was worked into a proper arrangement for *Rooster Rag*. Originally recorded in February 2011 and intended for the blues cover album that never came to fruition, 'Candyman Blues' was a favorite of Barrère's. ('I'd been listening to Mississippi John Hurt since I was thirteen. In fact, he's a major part of why I learned to play slide,' he gushed in the album's liner notes.) With the track's unabashed glee, 'wonderfully filthy' lyrics and stellar bottleneck work, it was the perfect album introduction.

'Rooster Rag' (Bill Payne, Robert Hunter)

The first of four Payne/Hunter co-writes, 'Rooster Rag' combines Payne's keen ear for melody with Hunter's lyrical absurdity: which taps beautifully into the spirit of Lowell George. Set to a jaunty bluegrass arrangement, the song is a full-on rag barnstormer, with Tackett blowing his trumpet while Larry Campbell saws away on fiddle. Payne's vocal is a little too relaxed at times, but that's appropriate to the spirit of the laid-back narrator, not wishing to impose his beliefs on others.

In 2012, Payne explained the writing process to dead.net:

I'd sit down and start to figure out where I'm going with it rhythmically and melodically and chordally, and then I came up to 'Tubal Cain was the god of fire/He got doused, first good rain,' and I thought, 'I've gotten this far with this song, and it's a rag, but I don't have any real ragtime chords in it,' so I thought, 'Tubal Cain' (*demonstrates on piano*), and came up with some changes that would reflect the ragtime ... I was scoring Hunter's lyrics. I almost had a visual on it.

'Church Falling Down' (Fred Tackett)

First recorded for Tackett's 2003 debut solo album *In a Town Like This*, this song was repurposed from a stark, sparse bluegrass into this atmospheric, swampy, earthy feel. It was inspired by a house of worship in disrepair,

129

that Tackett passed in Arkansas. He explained in the liner notes: 'I made a connection between all the vows that must have been said there, and how it was just like a divorce – all the things coming undone in life.' In the hands of Little Feat, the song evokes the spirit of Dr. John's debut album *Gris-Gris* (which Tackett acknowledged), with its groovy bass line, chattering percussion and soupy rhythm. Tackett's mandolin-playing accentuates his world-weary vocal, while the disembodied chorus vocals, chant and moan.

'Salome' (Bill Payne, Robert Hunter)

The highlight of both *Rooster Rag* and the Payne/Hunter collaboration is 'Salome': a simmering rocker that marries a zydeco influence and descriptive, mouthwatering lyrics. Payne later wrote of his newfound collaborator: 'Hunter's imagery is something that captured my imagination and played to one of my strengths: the visual. With 'Salome,' black-eyed peas, salty gravy and the gritty side of life is something I know.'

'Salome' stretches out over a luxurious six and a half minutes, with Gradney's propulsive bass and Ford's clattering drums keeping it moving. While Barrère and Larry Campbell drone away on bottleneck and fiddle, respectively, and Tackett picks away on mandolin, Payne unravels his story of the titular Jasper girl with the finest food around.

'One Breath At A Time' (Fred Tackett)

Ignore the intro's forced camaraderie (Tackett greets Clayton in a manner that reminds us why musicians aren't actors), and this track is a fun, funky rocker – extracted for reinvention from Tackett's 2010 solo album *Silver Strings*, to 'balance the Appalachian feel that we were putting into some of Bill's stuff with Hunter,' Tackett explained in the *Rooster Rag* liner notes. 'I started coaching Sam, and eventually, we got Paul involved too: kind of like three guys standing on a corner.'

The vocal trade-off is inspired, and the arrangement – with scorching guitar, whirling Hammond and Tackett's trumpet blasts – has all sorts of delightful little treats and surprises, with Barrère especially letting loose on guitar. It's a good reminder that Little Feat could still let down their hair and have some fun.

'Just A Fever' (Paul Barrère, Stephen Bruton)

Barrère and Hunter didn't co-write any songs for *Rooster Rag*, but Barrère did dig into his archives for this co-write with familiar Feats Auxiliary member Stephen Bruton: who'd co-written 'Corazones Y Sombras,' but passed from throat cancer in 2009. Barrère told *Marquee Magazine* in 2012:

> We had actually been friends for quite a while but had never written together. So when he came out to L.A., we got together at my house and we started these songs ... With 'Just A Fever,' we were kind of chuckling about, you know

– how we had a shared interest in the grape and the grain, probably to the excess, and how we managed to overcome that, and how do we get 'delirium tremens' into a song. We had this idea about 'just a fever,' and kind of a typical rock-and-roll love song, if you will. So it was just a great tagline for the chorus.

While Barrère and Bruton wrote several other songs, those were saved for the latter's solo projects, so 'Just A Fever' was Barrère's only song on the album. Considering that – and given the song is his last recorded and written for Little Feat – it's bittersweet to listen to. But more disappointing is that it's simply an average boogie rocker, with murky production and an odd doubling effect applied to Barrère's voice. However, it's still fun, and he especially ain't had enough yet; Ford and Gradney lock into a tenacious groove, Payne plinks away on piano and Barrère takes off on bottleneck: one of his fiercest performances on the album.

'Rag Top Down' (Bill Payne, Robert Hunter)
Hunter's lyrics are nothing if not evocative, and here he tapped into a youthful memory of Payne's without even realizing it. Payne explained in the liner notes: 'I'm from Texas, born there, and I spent my high school years in central California in Santa Maria, where I joined my first band at age fifteen. The guys in that band – The Debonairs – were low riders. Santa Maria was made for the culture of cruising. I was a surfer – another world, but my bandmates protected me. So, I knew the terrain.'

Payne wrote the music to Hunter's lyrics – the arrangement the closest to classic Little Feat. A gentle bridge borders on Payne's jazz-fusion excursions of old, while Ford channels Richie Hayward's spirit in his controlled yet ramshackle drum performance.

'Way Down Under' (Bill Payne, Robert Hunter)
The final Payne/Hunter co-write is also the most commercial, with its superb, rolling arrangement and Barrère's soaring bottleneck guitar. In a fair and just world, this would've been the album's radio hit for summer 2012. Payne noted in the liner notes that he 'didn't analyze Hunter's lyrics,' but only responded 'to certain words or phrases.' Uniquely, this was the only song of the four to start with the music instead of Hunter's lyrics: which are as light and airy as the performance.

'Jamaica Will Break Your Heart' (Fred Tackett)
Barrère sings lead on this rocker, taking on the role of a tourist wooed by Jamaican sun and herbs. The song was inspired by 'a guy named Thunder that we met when we started playing Jamaica,' Tackett explained in the liner notes. The song moves along at a quick clip – the Texicali Horns punctuating Ford's driving rhythm – before breaking down to halftime for the chorus. Tackett wove in an admonishment of Jamaican tourists ('A blue-eyed boy from 'cross

the sea/Erased our love and history'), lamenting in the album's liner notes that tourism 'brings in the dollars to Jamaica, but it interferes with the life of the Rasta culture, and that bothers me'; Barrère's resigned weariness indicating that no lessons have been, or will be, learned.

'Tattooed Girl' (Fred Tackett)

Tackett's fourth and final song is set to a sleazy, slinky shuffle – his sleepy vocal and muted trumpet giving a classic film noir feel. Originally, the music was written as an accompaniment to Tennessee Williams' poem 'Gold Tooth Blues,' but Tackett had difficulty securing the rights. He eventually wrote his own lyric: inspired by a Virginian waitress with a tattoo of the world on her shoulder, in a club the band had performed in. Having kicked off his 2010 album *Silver Strings* with a stripped-back acoustic arrangement of the song (with Tackett's son Miles on cello), Tackett here updated it for the full band. The track serves as a classy breather in between its lighthearted predecessor and scorching successor.

'The Blues Keep Coming' (Bill Payne, Gabe Ford)

The only *Rooster Rag* song that Payne wrote with someone other than Robert Hunter. Payne said it was inspired by 'Late winter in Montana, where I live, and that's the feeling of endless blues and endless cold.' Stuck for a third verse, he turned to Ford for assistance, 'which turned out very nicely.' The performance is a delightful slow burn, with Ford's take on the Purdie shuffle and Gradney's low rumbling bass providing the perfect foundation for Payne, Barrère and Tackett to build on. Barrère's slide guitar takes on an especially gritty tone.

'Mellow Down Easy' (Willie Dixon)

Rooster Rag – most likely Little Feat's final studio album – ends similarly to their final studio album with Lowell George: with Sam Clayton once again getting into the groove. It was recorded in February 2011 as part of the planned-but-abandoned blues-covers album. Written by Willie Dixon, 'Mellow Down Easy' was first recorded in 1954 by Little Walter and his Jukes: the version from which Little Feat drew their arrangement. It doesn't stray too far from the original. Fabulous Thunderbirds founder Kim Wilson blows away on harmonica, but the joy and bonhomie are palpable and closes this chapter of Little Feat's story nicely.

Postscript

Though Barrère was still writing and recording his own solo projects in his semi-retirement, he wasn't in as much of a rush to get back on the road, enjoying being at home and living comfortably, financially speaking. As far as Little Feat's future was concerned, he was non-committal. He told *jambands.com*:

> It's like, absence makes the heart grow fonder. Little Feat, for years and years, kept beating the same bushes. We noticed our guarantees were going down. It just wasn't a solid business plan. Nowadays, when we go to Jamaica and do four dates in the Northeast in the fall, people actually want to come see you, and in bigger venues. It works out as a better situation. There's talk of doing more than just the one fall run, but so far, nothing has come of it. Little Feat is always on the back burner. If it happens, it happens.

This blink-or-you'll-miss-us approach worked. 2017 and 2018 saw demand for more live shows, with six dates through the northeast added for May 2017 in addition to the four autumn dates, while the autumn residency was shifted to summer 2018 for an eight-date tour. It didn't take too long for the back burner to heat back up – Little Feat announced a 50th-anniversary tour for March 2019, with 28 dates taking them through most of North America, finishing on 8 June in Boulder, Colorado.

With the traditional autumn dates now expanded to a dozen, Barrère had every intention of joining Little Feat on 7 October in Minneapolis. But four days before, he announced on the band's website that he would have to bow out as his liver disease had returned. But he was optimistic he would return, ending his note with 'I have every intention of getting back to Jamaica in January, and rockin' on the beach with all of you. Until then, keep your sailin' shoes close by. If I have my way, you're going to need them!'

Sadly, Paul Barrère passed away on 26 October at UCLA Hospital. The band paid him tribute in the following statement:

> As the song he sang so many times put it, he was always 'Willin'', but it was not meant to be. Paul, sail on to the next place in your journey with our abiding love for a life always dedicated to the muse and the music. We are grateful for the time we have shared.

With two tour dates left, the band forged ahead, turning the Paramount show into an unofficial tribute for their fallen brother. Show opener 'Tripe Face Boogie' was dedicated to his memory, while Payne – who since Barrère's leave of absence at the start of the month, had taken over lead vocal duties on 'Willin'' – delivered an emotional, weathered performance of the longtime warhorse.

The tour wrapped up the following day in Wilkes-Barre, Pennsylvania, before the band went their separate ways. Both Payne and Tackett paid tribute to

Barrère on the band's website, with Tackett delivering a lovely instrumental classical guitar performance before offering a surprisingly-succinct message: 'Well, here's that rainy day. Goodbye, brother Paul. We rocked it. You were funky.' Meanwhile, Payne wrote a lengthy, poignant message from his home in Montana, concluding: 'I know well the intensity of who he was as a musician, as a man, and I honor that. My tears are of sadness, both for him and for those of us that knew him, that loved him, and that carry him in our hearts.'

It was a cruel and bitter irony celebrating 50 years of Little Feat, only to finish the tour with the death of one of the longest-serving members who was part of the creative force for nearly the same time span. The band's future remained uncertain until the end of November 2019, when Payne announced that their annual Jamaican Ramble On the Island dates would go forth as planned in January 2020. Scott Sharrard – who deputized for Barrère on the anniversary tour's last two dates – was brought in as a full-time member, and a host of musician friends joined them for a week-long party celebrating the life and music of Paul Barrère and Little Feat.

There were no concrete plans for 2020. On 7 March, Payne and Tackett joined the New Orleans Suspects at the Ardmore Music Hall, but nothing was set in stone. It was just as well, since the pandemic had pumped the brakes on live music. For a band like Little Feat who flourished on live performance, this would've spelled disaster. But considering 2019 was their first major tour in several years, the leaner years didn't necessarily affect the finances as drastically as they might've 30 years prior.

The same couldn't be said about crew members. While a band like Little Feat could afford to take a year off from live performance, their road crew typically would work with other bands, but their income source had completely dried up. The Rex Foundation – founded in 1983 by the Grateful Dead – created the Rex Roadie Fund in partnership with sweetrelief.org, 'to help ill, disabled and economically-challenged crew who are facing financial hardship.' During the pandemic, applications skyrocketed, so Little Feat jumped into action to help out.

In September 2020, a music video was released for an updated 'Long Distance Love': the message of which now took on an even more poignant tone. The new recording features Scott Sharrard on lead vocal and slide guitar, with drummer Tony Leone replacing Gabe Ford. It was released to raise awareness of the Rex Foundation's Roadie Fund (https://www.sweetrelief.org/ rex-roadie-fund.html), in partnership with Sweet Relief, whose goal is to help music crew members who are facing financial hardship. Payne wrote: 'The pandemic has decimated our industry. Those that do so much for bands day in and day out, are no longer working, and need our help. We are proud to do so. We ask that you give what you can.'

The following month, the first new Little Feat song in eight years debuted on YouTube, albeit as a work-in-progress mix, before finally being released in July 2021.

'When All Boats Rise' (Bill Payne, Tom Garnsey)

Produced by Bill Payne and Charles A. Martinez. Payne: vocal, keyboards; Gradney: bass; Clayton: percussion, vocals; Tackett; guitar, vocals; Scott Sharrard: guitar, vocals; Tony Leone: drums; Amy Helm and Catherine Russell: backing vocals. Rough version premiere: 26 October 2020; Digital single release: 16 July 2021

After moving to Montana in 2009, Payne struck up a friendship with Bozeman native Tom Garnsey, founder and guitarist/vocalist of Hooligans. Impressed with the band's sound, Payne would sit in on local gigs with them, and would co-produce and co-write with Garnsey three songs on their 2013 debut album *Beggars and Thieves*. Before long, Garnsey and Payne had a significant backlog of songs; one that Payne reserved for Little Feat was 'When All Boats Rise.' It was written in 2019, and Hooligans premiered it that December at Bozeman's The Filling Station, with Payne guesting on keyboards. This stirring call-to-arms for change in the wake of the worsening political climate since the American election of 2016 was recorded during the COVID-19 lockdown, and became even more prescient as the political and social events of 2020 unfolded. Payne wrote on the band's site:

This is a pivotal time for us all to pull together. As you listen to the words and reflect on the title of the song, you might understand why I feel it was important to get this out to you now. We need you to *go vote* ... John Lewis (former U.S. representative of Georgia and civil-rights activist who helped organize the 1963 March on Washington, among many other achievements) said we need to get in 'good trouble.'

'When All Boats Rise' is an effectively poignant and emotional song – Payne's weathered vocal suiting the lyric's weary resignation, while the chorus offers a hint of optimism. The arrangement borders a little too closely on the patriotic chest-thumping of the likes of 'Like A Rock' or 'Proud To Be An American,' but it's a pleasantly sanguine performance, distinguished by Tackett's ringing acoustic guitar and new drummer Tony Leone's steady backbeat. On the song's soft release in October 2020, Payne noted that the mix was a work in progress, and vocals and horns would be added. While backing vocals were provided by Amy Helm (daughter of Levon) and jazz singer Catherine Russell, horns were absent when the song was released the following July.

Little Feat announced the recommencement of live performances for November 2021, with the By Request tour – a short 17-date jaunt through New England and the South Atlantic United States, before returning to Jamaica in January: this time for Feat Camp 2022 (seemingly an event separate from Ramble On the Island). As for what the future holds for Little Feat, the losses of Richie Hayward and Paul Barrère were incalculable, but the band has always proven to be resilient.

Long may their shoes sail on.

Other releases: Live, compilation and solo albums
Live
Waiting for Columbus was considered such an untouchable representation of
Little Feat in concert, that it took until 1996 for them to release a follow-up. By
that time, they were on their fourth incarnation: with Craig Fuller gone, and one
studio album with Shaun Murphy already under their belt. *Live from Neon Park*
– recorded in December 1995 over five nights in Portland, San Francisco and
Hollywood – is a good representation of the Murphy-led Feats, with a handful of
friends (Piero Mariani and the Texicali Horns, Craig Fuller, Joel Tepp and Feats
progeny Inara George and Miles Tackett) showing up along the way. The album
was released to mild critical acclaim, but the demand for a live Little Feat album
was even less than for a studio album. A budget release – *Extended Versions:
The Encore Collection*: recorded at the El Rey Theatre in Los Angeles on 15 June
1998 – was released in 2000, and had a fairly even distribution of songs from
all three Little Feat eras, though distribution was significantly limited to truck
stops! Coupled with uninspired artwork and a misleading title that gave no
indication that the performances were live, the release failed miserably.

As such, the next live release wasn't until June 2002. *Raw Tomatos* and *Ripe
Tomatos* were two superb archival cross-sections of Little Feat live between
1971 and 2001 (though a separate, more concentrated focus on the Lowell
George years might've been more of a commercial success), released on their
own label Hot Tomato Records. (Highlights from the two were compiled into
2011's *The Hot Tomato Anthology*, which added a third disc of selections
from subsequent Hot Tomato live albums.) Five months later came *Live at
the Rams Head* – culled from six acoustic performances at Annapolis' Rams
Head club over three nights in June 2001. The following year, *Down Upon
the Suwannee River* (recorded on 21 October 2000 at the Spirit of Suwannee
River Musical Festival in Live Oak, Florida) and *Highwire Act: Live in St. Louis
2003* (recorded on 22 August 2003 at the Pageant in St. Louis, Missouri)
were released, the latter with an accompanying DVD courtesy of Eagle Rock
Entertainment. (That wasn't Little Feat's first DVD release. That honor goes to
2000's *Rockapalast Live* – reissued in 2009 as *Skin it Back: The Rockapalast
Collection*, which also featured a Barrère and Payne commentary, with special
guest Inara George stopping by for a quick chat.)

Two volumes of live performances called *Barnstormin'* were released in
2005, with the focus on lesser-known material – rarities like 'Changin' Luck,'
'Spider's Blues,' 'Walkin' As Two' and a cover of Little Walter's 'Last Night' on
the first volume; 'Fighting The Mosquito Wars,' 'Fool Yourself' and 'A Distant
Thunder' on the second – with a cover of 'Candyman Blues' predating its
studio recording by seven years. The following year, these two albums were
collected as a larger box set in a slipcase package, though there were no
additional tracks.

Rocky Mountain Jam was released in January 2007, and truly lives up to
its name: comprised of only six songs – recorded at the Boulder Theatre in

136

Colorado on 24 February 2006 – the album features three tracks clocking in at six minutes ('Marginal Creatures,' 'Rocket In My Pocket' and 'Feats Don't Fail Me Now'), and three exceeding ten minutes. 'One Clear Moment' approaches twelve, a medley of 'Spanish Moon' and 'Skin it Back' breezes past fifteen, and 'Dixie Chicken' clocks in at a whopping 21 minutes.

Three years later, Hot Tomato Records released the final archival live album *Rams Head Revisited*. The most recent live album, *Live In Holland 1976* was another Eagle Rock audio/visual combination: the audio being a complete show, while the video was absent of two songs ('One Love Stand' and 'Oh Atlanta').

There also exists a handful of *grey market* semi-legitimate releases with titles like *Late Night Truck Stop*, *Transmission Impossible*, *American Cutie* and *Hellzapoppin*. While I can't in good conscience recommend you spend hard-earned money on bootlegs, I *can* recommend you search for Little Feat on archive.org, where, with their blessing, the band's archivist Chris Cafiero has uploaded hundreds of top-quality Little Feat live shows from 1971 to the present day, all available for free.

The best-known bootleg *Electrif Lycanthrope* was one of the earliest bootlegs, taken from a radio performance for WLIR in Garden City, New York (recorded 19 September 1974 at Ultra-Sonic Studios), and one that Lowell George reportedly helped produce. In November 2021, the band's full set – minus 'Rock And Roll Doctor', which, the compilers explained, wasn't part of the original multitrack recordings – was released on vinyl and CD for Record Store Day (UK fans are forced to wait until June 2022, due to ongoing, worldwide supply chain shortages). If you can get it – copies are already going for inflated prices online – it's highly recommended.

Compilation

Discounting 1975's *Two Originals* – which was technically a reissue combining the debut album and *Dixie Chicken* for a reduced price – the first Little Feat compilation album was 1986's *As Time Goes By: The Best of Little Feat*: a twelve-track collection of favorites, released only in Europe. It was reissued in 1993, expanded to 20 tracks, but only in the UK. A vinyl remaster of the original was finally issued in the US in September 2016.

Two other attempts were made to capture Little Feat's career in a single-disc collection. 2005's *The Essentials* was a twelve-track sampler distributed only in Canada but made no real effort to dig deep, while 2006's *The Best of Little Feat* collected 17 tracks but made no attempt to be definitive.

However, the most comprehensive and essential compilation is 2000's *Hotcakes and Outtakes* – a four-disc box set consisting of two discs of material from the debut album through to *Hoy-Hoy!*; a third disc of the reformed Feats from 1988 to 1998, and a fourth disc of outtakes from sessions between 1969 and 1979. With its remastered sound, the occasional rare single, and fascinating insight from Bud Scoppa, the box set is a must-have for any Feats fan.

Some other box sets have snuck out since, though they were mostly for those on a budget. 2010's *Original Album Series* compiled the first five albums as mini-LPs in a cardboard box; 2012's *The Triple Album Collection* compiled *Dixie Chicken*, *The Last Record Album* and *Time Loves a Hero*, and 2014's *Rad Gumbo: The Complete Warner Bros. Years 1971-1990* compiled exactly that, with a bonus disc: *Outtakes from Hotcakes*.

Solo

It would be incorrect and unfair to say the only worthy solo album from a Little Feat member was Lowell George's *Thanks, I'll Eat It Here*. Both Paul Barrère and Bill Payne have released solid albums, Fred Tackett's solo albums on Hot Tomato Records are worth checking out, and Shaun Murphy's solo career continues to this day. Payne's debut solo album – 2005's *Cielo Norte* – is entirely instrumental and almost entirely self-performed. While he promised further albums, it seems his interests lie elsewhere – primarily in his excellent photography – and his solo career is on ice for the time being.

Barrère's solo career yielded a little more music. His first two efforts – 1983's *On My Own Two Feet* and 1984's *Real Lies* – are enjoyable if ultimately forgettable. If you're dying to get the best of the best, you can't go wrong with Zoo Entertainment's 1995 compilation *If the Phone Don't Ring*, though both albums are relatively cheap on reputable sites, and if streaming is more your thing, they're both available on Apple Music and Spotify. Barrère then formed The Bluesbusters with Catfish Hodge and T. Lavitz, releasing *Accept No Substitutes* in 1986 and *This Time* in 1987, before breaking up. Subsequent solo efforts include collaborations with Roger Cole on *Riding the Nova Train*, *Musical Schizophrenia* and *Lost In the Sound*.

In 1993, Frank Zappa's Bizarre Records issued *Lightning-Rod Man*: a fifteen-track compilation of recordings by The Factory. Except for the previously-released cover of 'Framed,' Lowell George wrote or co-wrote all the songs. They're all decent compositions and performances, but very much of the mid-1960s California atonal *freak-out* sound. As a curiosity, the album is an interesting listen, but not worth many repeats.

Reissues

Unfortunately, Little Feat's back catalog is a shambles, with their albums spread across multiple record labels, with no attempts made to cohesively reissue anything. If any CDs are available, they're usually the mid-1980s reissues, though *The Last Record Album* was inexplicably remastered and reissued in 2012 (with relevant bonus tracks taken from the *Hotcakes* box set). That same year, *Time Loves a Hero* and *Down on the Farm* were paired up for a 2-for-1 CD release. But except for the exhaustive 2002 *Waiting for Columbus* reissue, Little Feat's discography has largely been forgotten and neglected, with a complete overhaul sorely overdue. Maybe someday.

Resources and further reading

Books and liner notes

Barrère, P., Liner notes for *Let It Roll* (Warner Bros. Records, 1988), *Representing the Mambo* (Warner Bros. Records, 1990), *Shake Me Up* (Morgan Creek Records, 1991), *Ain't Had Enough Fun* (Zoo Records, 1995), *Under the Radar* (CMC International, 1998), *Chinese Work Songs* (CMC International, 2000), *Raw Tomatos Vol. 1* and *Ripe Tomatos Vol. 1* (Hot Tomato Records, 2002), *Kickin' It at the Barn* (Hot Tomato Records, 2003)
Brend, M., *Rock and Roll Doctor* (Backbeat Books, 2002)
Feat, L. *et al*, Liner notes for *Hoy-Hoy!* (Warner Bros. Records, 1981)
Fong-Torres, B., *Willin': The Story of Little Feat* (Da Capo Press, 2013)
McNally, D., Liner notes for *Rooster Rag* (Hot Tomato Records, 2012)
Payne, B., Liner notes for *Kickin' It at the Barn* (Hot Tomato Records, 2003), *Join the Band* (429 Records, 2008), *Rooster Rag* (Hot Tomato Records, 2012)
Scoppa, B., Liner notes for *Hotcakes and Outtakes* (Rhino, 2000), *Waiting for Columbus* (Rhino expanded edition, 2002)

Articles and Interviews

Noted as applicable in text.

Internet

www.littlefeat.net
www.featbase.net
www.featphotos.net
archive.org/details/LittleFeat
www.youtube.com/user/LittleFeatArchive
www.paulandfred.net
www.billpaynecreative.com
www.facebook.com/LittleFeat

On Track series

Tori Amos – Lisa Torem 978-1-78952-142-9

Asia – Peter Braidis 978-1-78952-099-6

Barclay James Harvest – Keith and Monica Domone 978-1-78952-067-5

The Beatles – Andrew Wild 978-1-78952-009-5

The Beatles Solo 1969-1980 – Andrew Wild 978-1-78952-030-9

Blue Oyster Cult – Jacob Holm-Lupo 978-1-78952-007-1

Marc Bolan and T.Rex – Peter Gallagher 978-1-78952-124-5

Kate Bush – Bill Thomas 978-1-78952-097-2

Camel – Hamish Kuzminski 978-1-78952-040-8

Caravan – Andy Boot 978-1-78952-127-6

Cardiacs – Eric Benac 978-1-78952-131-3

Eric Clapton Solo – Andrew Wild 978-1-78952-141-2

The Clash – Nick Assirati 978-1-78952-077-4

Crosby, Stills and Nash – Andrew Wild 978-1-78952-039-2

The Damned – Morgan Brown 978-1-78952-136-8

Deep Purple and Rainbow 1968-79 – Steve Pilkington 978-1-78952-002-6

Dire Straits – Andrew Wild 978-1-78952-044-6

The Doors – Tony Thompson 978-1-78952-137-5

Dream Theater – Jordan Blum 978-1-78952-050-7

Elvis Costello and The Attractions – Georg Purvis 978-1-78952-129-0

Emerson Lake and Palmer – Mike Goode 978-1-78952-000-2

Fairport Convention – Kevan Furbank 978-1-78952-051-4

Peter Gabriel – Graeme Scarfe 978-1-78952-138-2

Genesis – Stuart MacFarlane 978-1-78952-005-7

Gentle Giant – Gary Steel 978-1-78952-058-3

Gong – Kevan Furbank 978-1-78952-082-8

Hawkwind – Duncan Harris 978-1-78952-052-1

Roy Harper – Opher Goodwin 978-1-78952-130-6

Iron Maiden – Steve Pilkington 978-1-78952-061-3

Jefferson Airplane – Richard Butterworth 978-1-78952-143-6

Jethro Tull – Jordan Blum 978-1-78952-016-3

Elton John in the 1970s – Peter Kearns 978-1-78952-034-7

The Incredible String Band – Tim Moon 978-1-78952-107-8

Iron Maiden – Steve Pilkington 978-1-78952-061-3

Judas Priest – John Tucker 978-1-78952-018-7

Kansas – Kevin Cummings 978-1-78952-057-6

Led Zeppelin – Steve Pilkington 978-1-78952-151-1

Level 42 – Matt Philips 978-1-78952-102-3

Aimee Mann – Jez Rowden 978-1-78952-036-1

Joni Mitchell – Peter Kearns 978-1-78952-081-1

The Moody Blues – Geoffrey Feakes 978-1-78952-042-2

Mike Oldfield – Ryan Yard 978-1-78952-060-6

Tom Petty – Richard James 978-1-78952-128-3

Porcupine Tree – Nick Holmes 978-1-78952-144-3

Queen – Andrew Wild 978-1-78952-003-3

Radiohead – William Allen 978-1-78952-149-8

Renaissance – David Detmer 978-1-78952-062-0

The Rolling Stones 1963-80 – Steve Pilkington 978-1-78952-017-0

The Smiths and Morrissey – Tommy Gunnarsson 978-1-78952-140-5

Steely Dan – Jez Rowden 978-1-78952-043-9

Steve Hackett – Geoffrey Feakes 978-1-78952-098-9

Thin Lizzy – Graeme Stroud 978-1-78952-064-4

Toto – Jacob Holm-Lupo 978-1-78952-019-4

U2 – Eoghan Lyng 978-1-78952-078-1

UFO – Richard James 978-1-78952-073-6

The Who – Geoffrey Feakes 978-1-78952-076-7

Roy Wood and the Move – James R Turner 978-1-78952-008-8

Van Der Graaf Generator – Dan Coffey 978-1-78952-031-6

Yes – Stephen Lambe 978-1-78952-001-9

Frank Zappa 1966 to 1979 – Eric Benac 978-1-78952-033-0

10CC – Peter Kearns 978-1-78952-054-5

Decades Series

The Bee Gees in the 1960s – Andrew Mon Hughes et al 978-1-78952-148-1

Alice Cooper in the 1970s – Chris Sutton 978-1-78952-104-7

Curved Air in the 1970s – Laura Shenton 978-1-78952-069-9

Fleetwood Mac in the 1970s – Andrew Wild 978-1-78952-105-4

Focus in the 1970s – Stephen Lambe 978-1-78952-079-8

Genesis in the 1970s – Bill Thomas 978178952-146-7

Marillion in the 1980s – Nathaniel Webb 978-1-78952-065-1

Pink Floyd In The 1970s – Georg Purvis 978-1-78952-072-9

The Sweet in the 1970s – Darren Johnson 978-1-78952-139-9

Uriah Heep in the 1970s – Steve Pilkington 978-1-78952-103-0

Yes in the 1980s – Stephen Lambe with David Watkinson 978-1-78952-125-2

On Screen series

Carry On... – Stephen Lambe 978-1-78952-004-0

David Cronenberg – Patrick Chapman 978-1-78952-071-2

Doctor Who: The David Tennant Years – Jamie Hailstone 978-1-78952-066-8

Monty Python – Steve Pilkington 978-1-78952-047-7

Seinfeld Seasons 1 to 5 – Stephen Lambe 978-1-78952-012-5

James Bond – Andrew Wild 978-1-78952-010-1

Other Books

Babysitting A Band On The Rocks – G.D. Praetorius 978-1-78952-106-1

Derek Taylor: For Your Radioactive Children – Andrew Darlington 978-1-78952-038-5

Iggy and The Stooges On Stage 1967-1974 – Per Nilsen 978-1-78952-101-6

Jon Anderson and the Warriors – the road to Yes – David Watkinson 978-1-78952-059-0

Nu Metal: A Definitive Guide – Matt Karpe 978-1-78952-063-7

Tommy Bolin: In and Out of Deep Purple – Laura Shenton 978-1-78952-070-5

Maximum Darkness – Deke Leonard 978-1-78952-048-4

Maybe I Should've Stayed In Bed – Deke Leonard 978-1-78952-053-8

Psychedelic Rock in 1967 – Kevan Furbank 978-1-78952-155-9

The Twang Dynasty – Deke Leonard 978-1-78952-049-1

and many more to come!

Would you like to write for Sonicbond Publishing?

We are mainly a music publisher, but we also occasionally publish in other genres including film and television. At Sonicbond Publishing we are always on the look-out for authors, particularly for our two main series, On Track and Decades.

Mixing fact with in depth analysis, the On Track series examines the entire recorded work of a particular musical artist or group. All genres are considered from easy listening and jazz to 60s soul to 90s pop, via rock and metal.

The Decades series singles out a particular decade in an artist or group's history and focuses on that decade in more detail than may be allowed in the On Track series.

While professional writing experience would, of course, be an advantage, the most important qualification is to have real enthusiasm and knowledge of your subject. First-time authors are welcomed, but the ability to write well in English is essential.

Sonicbond Publishing has distribution throughout Europe and North America, and all our books are also published in E-book form. Authors will be paid a royalty based on sales of their book. Further details about our books are available from www.sonicbondpublishing.com. To contact us, complete the contact form there or email info@sonicbondpublishing.co.uk